Random Ramblings of a Raving Redhead

Dana Rongione

Random Ramblings of a Raving Redhead

Published by

On-Demand Publishing, LLC

All Scripture notations are taken from
The Holy Bible, KJV

Copyright 2010 – Dana Rongione

Cover illustration by Tim Williams

ISBN - 1452862818
EAN-13 - 9781452862811

ACKNOWLEDGEMENTS

Jason - You are the best husband any woman could ever dream of. Thank you for your constant help, support, and willingness to be a part of so many of my stories. But most of all, thanks for always having a listening ear. I love you!

My family - You have been supportive of my efforts and have helped and encouraged me in so many ways. Thanks for believing in me!

My church family - It is such a great joy to have so many great friends with whom I can share this accomplishment. Thanks for your friendship, and your excitement. Preacher Mark, thanks for the many ideas you gave me through your sermons. If some devotions sound familiar. . .well, I'm sure you understand.

Aunt Tracy - You have no idea how much I appreciate your editing services. What a privilege for me to have such a talented aunt! Thanks for all your hard work.

TABLE OF CONTENTS

HAPPILY EVER AFTER

Sometimes I feel like a character in a fairy tale. I don't have a wicked stepmother, but sometimes I do feel like a prisoner held captive by my fears and doubts. I haven't eaten any poison apples lately, but I have tasted the acrid flavor of Satan's lies time and time again. I don't recall pricking my finger on any spinning wheels, but I have felt the pain of rejection and betrayal. I've never bought any magic beans, but I, too, have made unwise investments that are still seeking to destroy me.

I've heard it said that fairy tales are not good for us. Some say that they completely misrepresent reality and cause us to be discontent with our mediocre existence. Have they read any fairy tales recently? I can't think of a single one that I would want to be part of, can you? Chased by wolves, giants, and wicked queens? No, thank you!

I, for one, think there's a lot more reality to fairy tales than some would like to believe. No, I'm not saying that I believe in fairies or anything like that. I'm just saying that there are some valuable lessons to be learned. But some argue that there is no such thing as "happily ever after" and that saying the contrary simply leads people to future disappointment. I respectfully disagree. There is a "happily ever after." My Bible says so.

I know without a shadow of a doubt that I am going to Heaven someday. Whether it be by way of the rapture or by death, I know that I'm going. I also know that Heaven is a wonderful place. There is no death, no sickness, and no crying. There is joy and happiness. There is peace and tranquility. There are no strangers in Heaven, neither is there sin. But most of all, Jesus will be there. Oh, yes, Heaven is a wonderful place, and I'm going. So, you see, no matter how bad things seem sometimes here on earth, my story will end happily ever after. Actually, I take that back. My story won't end. It will continue for all eternity. . . happily ever after.

Then we which are alive and remain shall be caught up together with them in the clouds, to meet the Lord in the air: and so shall we ever be with the Lord. - 1 Thessalonians 4:17

THOUGHTS, THOUGHTS, WHEREFORE ART THOU?

Psalm 139 says, *O Lord, thou hast searched me, and known me, , thou understandest my thought afar off.* Now, I know that the meaning of this verse is that God understands our thoughts even from Heaven, but the other day, I saw another possible meaning.

I was having my daily devotions, and for the life of me, I could not keep my mind focused. My thoughts were wandering all over the place. After repeating the same prayer request for the third time, I got really frustrated with myself, and the Lord brought Psalm 139 to my mind. I laughed. The way I look at it is that it's not only God who is afar off, it's my thoughts as well. They're way out there, but even then, the Lord understands. He knows what I mean to say and what I'm trying to express, even though many times I feel that I don't know myself. He understands my thoughts, even when they are not focused where they should be.

Don't get me wrong. I'm not advocating letting our thoughts run wild all the time. I'm just saying that it's good to know that during those times when our thoughts seem out of control and out of our grasp, the Lord knows and understands. What a great God we serve!

Search me, O God, and know my heart; try me, and know my thoughts. - Psalm 139:23

STOP AND SMELL THE SKUNK?

On our way to church Sunday morning, we ran over a skunk. We came up over the hill, and there he was lying in the road. We didn't have time to swerve and miss him. Needless to say, it was a VERY long ride to church. We rolled the windows down, hoping that the fresh outside air would help to get rid of some of the smell. We noticed that as long as we were moving, the smell wasn't too bad. If we stopped, however, the fragrance was overwhelming. It stunk so bad that I could taste it. In fact, it was so bad that I was afraid my clothes were going to start smelling skunk-like as well. So we did our best to keep moving. . .that is, until we got to church. (I won't even go into the smell that awaited us when we got out of church that afternoon. Let's just say it wasn't pleasant.)

You know, sometimes life stinks. Things happen that we feel shouldn't. Daily circumstances don't always meet our qualifications for a good day. All in all, it stinks just like the skunk we hit (may he rest in pieces—er—peace). But if we sit around thinking about how bad things are, the smell (or circumstance) won't get any better. In fact, it will get worse. The best way to deal with the smell is to keep moving. Keep going. Keep running the race. Keep serving the Lord. Don't focus on the smell, focus on doing all you can to please the Lord. As we do, the smell starts to wear off to the point that we hardly notice it anymore. Praise the Lord!

(BTW, if you're riding down 183 towards Pickens any time in the near future, watch out for Pepe La Pew! He's hard to miss.)

For God is not unrighteous to forget your work and labour of love, which ye have shewed toward his name, in that ye have ministered to the saints, and do minister. And we desire that every one of you do shew the same diligence to the full assurance of hope unto the end. - Hebrews 6:10-11

WHEN THERE IS NONE

When reading through the book of Isaiah, I admit that a lot of it goes completely over my head. I have to be very careful when I read passages like this because I find myself reading the words without really paying attention to what I'm reading. When I catch myself doing this, I make myself go back and read it again.

Every now and then, there is a verse or two that just jump off the page. I don't know why or how, but some verses reach out and grab me. The verse that really got my attention this morning was Isaiah 41:17. *When the poor and needy seek water, and there is none, and their tongue faileth for thirst, I the LORD will hear them, I the God of Israel will not forsake them.*

In our day, we have no idea what it means to be truly thirsty. I know I often say, "I'm about to die of thirst," but the truth is we are blessed and have no idea what it's like to go without water. But, I don't think this verse is just talking about water. I think it's talking about anything we may need. I don't think it would be harming the Scripture if we inserted another word in place of the word "water."

When the poor and needy seek money, and there is none. . .l the LORD will hear them, l the God of Israel will not forsake them.

When the poor and needy seek peace, and there is none. . .l the LORD will hear them, l the God of Israel will not forsake them.

When the poor and needy seek acceptance, and there is none. . .l the LORD will hear them, l the God of Israel will not forsake them.

When the poor and needy seek love, and there is none. . .l the LORD will hear them, l the God of Israel will not forsake them.

When the poor and needy seek employment, and there is none. . .l the LORD will hear them, l the God of Israel will not forsake them.*

When the poor and needy seek companionship, and there is none. . .l the LORD will hear them, l the God of Israel will not forsake them.

There are many words that we could fill in right there. Perhaps you even have one that describes what you are needing right now. The point is that no matter what we need, the Lord will hear our cries, and He will not forsake us. He has our best interest at heart. He will meet our needs in His own time. Our job is simply to trust Him.

*NOTE: At the time I wrote this, my husband was getting laid off from his job. I had no idea! God was speaking to me before I knew I needed to hear it. That's how faithful He is!

PRIDE AND PASTURES

All this came upon the king Nebuchadnezzar. At the end of twelve months he walked in the palace of the kingdom of Babylon. The king spake, and said, Is not this great Babylon, that I have built for the house of the kingdom by the might of my power, and for the honour of my majesty? While the word was in the king's mouth, there fell a voice from heaven, saying, O king Nebuchadnezzar, to thee it is spoken; The kingdom is departed from thee. And they shall drive thee from men, and thy dwelling shall be with the beasts of the field: they shall make thee to eat grass as oxen, and seven times shall pass over thee, until thou know that the most High ruleth in the kingdom of men, and giveth it to whomsoever he will. The same hour was the thing fulfilled upon Nebuchadnezzar: and he was driven from men, and did eat grass as oxen, and his body was wet with the dew of heaven, till his hairs were grown like eagles' feathers, and his nails like birds' claws. - Daniel 4:28-33

Okay, how many of us have done the same thing as Nebuchadnezzar did? How many of us have taken credit for something the Lord did? Hmmm. Tough question, huh? The truth is we all have a pride problem from time to time. Whether it's taking credit for things that God accomplished or thinking that we're always right, pride is a sin, and a very dangerous one at that.

Aren't you glad, though, that God doesn't always punish pride the way He did in this story? I don't know if Nebuchadnezzar turned into a mad man for a while or if he actually turned into a beast, but I do know that his life was miserable during that time. I know that God showed him Who was really in control.

The really bad part about this story is that Nebuchadnezzar knew it was coming. God had warned him in a dream, and Daniel had interpreted that dream. All Nebuchadnezzar had to do was heed the warning, and the whole thing would have never happened.

We, too, have been warned about pride. The Bible is full of verses that remind us that pride is wrong and something that the Lord despises. It warns us that destruction follows on the heels of pride. Even Nebuchadnezzar, after his ordeal, warns us of pride. Pay close attention to the last verse of this chapter.

Now I Nebuchadnezzar praise and extol and honour the King of heaven, all whose works are truth, and his ways judgment: and those that walk in pride he is able to abase.

Will we heed the warnings or will we ignore them like Nebuchadnezzar and face the consequences? I don't know about you, but I don't care much for grazing, so I think I'll heed the warnings!

NOT THE BRIGHTEST CRAYON

My husband, Jason, and I often take our two dogs out walking at a nearby lake named Lake Wattacoo. It is a secluded place that consists of two or three different trails, a small lake, a distant waterfall, etc. It's really a beautiful destination, and because it is secluded, we find that it's a good place to go to "get away from the world." (Plus, the dogs really enjoy it.)

At one point, there is a fork in the trail that leads out of the woods. Our older dog, Tippy, is precious, but not the brightest crayon in the box, if you know what I mean. She constantly takes the wrong side of the fork, and the bad part is that she doesn't realize she's going the wrong way. I think, in her mind, she sees that we're headed in the same general direction and so assumes the trails must lead to the same place. What she doesn't know is that a little farther along her trail, the path turns and basically leads back to where we just came from. So each time she goes that way, we have to call her and once again convince her that she's going the wrong way and to trust us because we know what's best. Many times, she'll ignore our warnings, only to find herself alone, turned around, and headed in the wrong direction. That's when she starts running back in an attempt to catch up with us.

Just like Tippy, I am sometimes not the brightest crayon in the box. I try to do things my own way in my own strength. My ultimate goal is the glory of the Lord, but I try to accomplish this through my own devices instead of the way He has set up for me to follow. Just like Tippy, I am convinced that since the paths are headed in the same direction, they must end up in the same place. I, too, am often certain that my way is better or easier. And unfortunately, I often ignore the warnings of the Master that I am on the wrong path. Instead, I plod along my trail, allowing the Master to get farther and farther from my view, until I find myself alone and unsure how I came to be back at the place where I started. Oh, if only I would heed the direction of the Master. It would save me from re-walking a lot of trails!

Teach me thy way, O LORD, and lead me in a plain path, because of mine enemies. - Psalm 27:11

THERE IS A SEASON

I am quickly coming to the conclusion that hiking is not nearly as enjoyable in the summer as it is the rest of the year. In the fall and spring, I love nothing more than to hike a trail to a remote waterfall or follow along beside a babbling brook. I love to sit and bask in the sunshine as I rest and listen to the water's peaceful flow. It is a tranquility like nothing else.

In the winter, the cool weather is perfect for those strenuous climbs where I find myself shedding layer after layer until I'm finally down to my t-shirt. And even though the scenery is not as vibrant, there is a certain beauty in the quiet woods that are at rest.

Hiking in the summer is a different story entirely. It's HOT!!! The grass, weeds, and briers are in abundance and love nothing better than to grab at my legs. The bears are out of their slumber (thankfully, I haven't seen any of them yet). The snakes are slithering around, hissing at any who dare pass by (unfortunately, I've seen plenty of these). Every other step I take, I find myself wrapped up in a sticky spiderweb. And then, there are the bugs. Let me tell you, there is not an insect repellent on earth that will keep gnats out of your face. They fly in my eyes, my mouth, my nose, my ears, and anywhere else they can find. And if that weren't bad enough, the mosquitoes bite, the ticks grab hold, and the bees sting. Trust me, I've experienced them all this summer. So, with all these annoyances and irritations, I find that hiking in the summer is just not very enjoyable at all.

Life, too, has seasons. There are seasons full of beauty and tranquility. However, there are also seasons full of irritations and obstacles that sap the joy out of the journey. During these times, it is important to focus on the good times of the journey and to know that seasons of peace and joy are right around the corner if only we will remain faithful. Yes, it's hard. Yes, it's discouraging. But it is worth it. We can't give up on the journey just because of a tough season. Think of all the blessings we'll miss when those good seasons roll in again.

So, put on your sunscreen and your insect repellent. Fill up the water bottles, and let's keep hiking! As for snakes, I've found that they really seem to be more scared of me than I am of them. Go figure!

To every thing there is a season, and a time to every purpose under the heaven. - Ecclesiastes 3:1

FIGHTING FOR SPIRITUAL FOOD

My parents were out of town last week, so their dog spent the time with us. Let me tell you, three dogs in one small house is quite a crowd. Cocoa is usually very whiny when he spends time with us. He likes us, but he misses his house and his "daddy" plus I think he knows that my dog, Mitch, doesn't like him very much. You have to understand Mitch. He's a sweet and precious dog, but he's also very protective, especially of me. He doesn't like another dog coming in and messing with his "mommy."

Tippy, my beagle mix, is very easy-going. She'll do whatever. She doesn't care who's there and who isn't there. As long as she has her food, she's happy. All in all, I was proud of all the dogs this past week. Cocoa didn't whine, and Mitch didn't fuss. . .until the last day.

I was trying to fix dinner for all three dogs. I had their bowls on the table, and I was dishing out food for each. I went to the kitchen to get something, and the war broke out. Cocoa had sniffed at the wrong bowl. He had the nerve to put his nose close to Mitch's bowl. That was the only excuse Mitch needed to "set Cocoa straight." (What can I say? My dog is a bully!)

My attempts to break up the fight were not working, so Jason stepped in and grabbed Mitch. Cocoa ran in the opposite direction. (Smart dog!) Mitch was given a firm reprimand for being so grouchy, and Cocoa's minor wounds were tended to.

As I explained to Jason what had happened, I was reminded of the attacks of Satan. He doesn't want us to get our food either—spiritual food, that is. Have you ever noticed as soon as you sit down to a spiritual meal in the form of prayer, Bible reading, or worship time, he attacks? The phone rings. The oven timer goes off. The drier buzzes. Our minds wander. Our eyes grow heavy. Just as Mitch attacked Cocoa for going near his food, so will Satan attack as we near our spiritual food. How will we respond to his attack? Will we, like Cocoa, run the other way, or will we stay and fight? Just some food for thought today. (Pardon the pun!)

Wherefore take unto you the whole armour of God, that ye may be able to withstand in the evil day, and having done all, to stand - Ephesians 6:13

IF ONLY. . .

If only my husband hadn't been laid off. . .
If only there were enough money to pay
the bills. . .
If only my writing were more profitable. . .
If only the car hadn't been damaged. . .
If only things around the house worked like
they're supposed to. . .
If only the pain in my shoulder would go away. . .

If only, if only, if only. If only all these things
were so, it would be easy to rejoice in the Lord.
Don't you think? If life were smooth and simple,
wouldn't it be easy to sing praises?

According to Philippians 4:4, however, we're
supposed to rejoice in the Lord, no matter the
circumstances.

Rejoice in the Lord always; and again I say, Rejoice.

What? How can I rejoice in the midst of so many
heartaches? How can I praise the Lord when so
many things are going wrong? How can I stay in a
constant state of rejoicing? I think the answer
can be found in the next few verses.

Let your moderation be known unto all men. The Lord is at hand. Be careful for nothing; but in every thing by prayer and supplication with thanksgiving let your requests be made known unto God. And the peace of God, which passeth all understanding, shall keep your hearts and minds through Christ Jesus. Finally, brethren, whatsoever things are true, whatsoever things are honest, whatsoever things are just, whatsoever things are pure, whatsoever things are lovely, whatsoever things are of good report; if there be any virtue, and if there be any praise, think on these things. Those things, which ye have both learned, and received, and heard, and seen in me, do: and the God of peace shall be with you. - Philippians 4:5-9

Scofield calls this "the secret of the peace of God." Do you want to be able to rejoice at all times and in all circumstances? According to the above passage, here's what you need to do:

1. Don't worry
2. Take it to God in prayer
3. Be thankful
4. Think positive
5. Consistently do what you've learned

Another thing that will help us is to focus on Christ, not the crisis. (That goes along with "think positive," but I wanted to mention it anyway.) Sure, life looks rough if I'm only looking at all the things that are going wrong. But if I will focus on the many blessings around me, I will be more likely to rejoice. Let's get rid of the "if only's." They are time-wasters and energy-drainers. Instead, let's put our time and energy to a good use--praising the Lord Who is worthy of our praise!

COMFORT IN CLOSENESS

One topic that I come across often in devotional books is how to draw closer to Jesus. It has been discussed from many pulpits and in countless conferences. The advice given ranges from complete and total surrender to Christ to completing the work He has sent us here to do. Often, the advice is helpful, but sometimes the answers are so complex. Should it be that way?

My advice on the topic is that you draw closer to Jesus in the same way that you grow closer to your friends or family. You spend time with Him. You talk with Him and listen as He speaks to you. You share your cares, burdens, and joys with Him. You laugh and cry with Him. You work through things together and complete tasks in the company of one another. You learn more about Him and in turn, allow yourself to be known.

Treat Him like the Friend that He is. Rely on Him like the Father He is. It may sound simple, but I think that's the way God intended it. We are often guilty of over-complicating things. Do you want to be closer to Christ today? It is possible, but some time and effort on your part are required.

Draw nigh unto God, and he will draw nigh to you - James 4:8a

THE BIRD AND THE BRE

I saw the funniest thing this past Sat<
was cleaning up the fellowship building   _i
church after brunch. As I pushed the broom past
the window, I stopped. A huge black bird was in
the yard. His mouth was full of the toast that we
had thrown out. It was really a comical sight—
this black bird with a mouth full of white toast.
And his mouth was completely full. The toast was
sticking out of each side of his beak. It was
hilarious.

The thing that caught my attention next was
that he kept trying to pick up more of the toast.
"Don't be greedy," I heard myself saying. But he
didn't listen. He tried in vain over and over again
to pick up another piece of toast, but his beak
was just too full. Finally, in frustration, he put
his mouthful down on the ground and picked up
the single piece that was giving him so much
trouble. Then he tried to pick up the mouthful
again. It didn't work. After several minutes, he
flew off with the single piece in his beak, leaving
the mouthful on the ground. Stupid bird!

ut then I started thinking. We're the same way, aren't we? We go through life always trying to get more. Maybe we're not all striving for more possessions, but how about more time, more energy, or better health? Just like the black bird, our lives are full of blessings, but in frustration, we set them all aside so that we can pick up one more thing. We fool ourselves into thinking we can have it all, but just like the bird, we find that we can't handle all those blessings at one time.

It would do us all good to remember the black bird. Let's not sacrifice all of today's blessings because of greed. Let's take today's blessings and enjoy them. God will send more when we need them. Let us be content with what we have and raise our voices to Heaven as we say, "We have enough!"

And God is able to make all grace abound toward you; that ye, always having all sufficiency in all things, may abound to every good work - II Corinthians 9:8

STARTING OVER AGAIN

It's that time of year again. That's right. It's time to clean out the pool. Now, I don't have a pool, but my sister and her husband do. In fact, he's been working on getting that pool clean for a couple of weeks now. The dirt is out. The debris is out. The water, however, is still a rather disturbing shade of green. He's put enough shock in the water that anything in it should have keeled over and died by now. Yet the water remains green. He finally decided that the only way the pool was going to be ready in time for summer was to drain the water out and start all over again.

This reminds me of salvation. You see, before salvation, our lives were full of dirt, debris, and other things that were keeping us from being what we should be. We tried earthly remedies, but still, our lives didn't clear up. The murkiness continued to surround us.

When we allowed Jesus to come into our lives, He cleaned us the only way possible. He dumped out the old and filled us with the new. In essence, He started all over again. We were born again. We became new creatures in Christ.

One difference between the pool and salvation is that the pool can become murky again. (Sorry, Bryan!) Our lives, though full of trials and troubles, can never go back to the state that they were once in. We can never return to that life. No, we are forever changed!

Therefore if any man be in Christ, he is a new creature: old things are passed away; behold, all things are become new. - II Corinthians 5:17

THE PLANT WHISPERER

I don't have much of a green thumb. In fact, I can guarantee you that if I receive a plant of any kind, it will be dead within 72 hours. Giving me a plant is like condemning it to death. I once had someone give me a miniature rose bush. She assured me that I could not kill it. "Just put it in the ground where it can get both sun and shade, and it will grow." I followed her instructions. The poor thing didn't stand a chance. It was dead within the week. Plants are not my thing!

One thing I do know about plants is that they require two things: water and sunshine. Without these essential elements, the plant will wither and die. With them, the plant can thrive and grow, often times producing fruit.

The Christian life is the same way, for it, too, requires two things: the Bible and prayer. Without them, the Christian life will wither and die. With them, the Christian can thrive and grow, often times producing fruit. Isn't the similarity astounding?

Another similarity between plants and Christians is that it takes time for "the seed" to grow into what it's meant to be. When you first plant a seed, it may be weeks or even months before you see any evidence of change in that seed. You've watered it. You've given it plenty of sun. But still, you see no results. (In my case, that's probably because I've already killed it, but for the rest of you, this is a normal stage in the process of growth.) Sometimes the Christian life is that way. We read our Bible and pray, but we still don't see the growth we long for. Just as with the plant, what we don't see is the change that is occurring under the surface.

Are you frustrated today because you don't see the growth in your Christian walk that you would like to see? Are you questioning your usefulness because it seems that you haven't made a difference in this world? Are you despairing of ever seeing fruit for your labors? If so, I beg of you, don't quit taking care of your seed. Nourish it. Water it with the Word. Expose it to the light of God's truth and goodness. And then, when you least expect it, you'll see the beginnings of the growth you've longed for. But be warned. If you forsake the care of your seed, it will wither and die. The choice is yours. Choose wisely!

But grow in grace, and in the knowledge of our Lord and Saviour Jesus Christ. To him be glory both now and for ever. Amen. - II Peter 3:18

HOW FIRM IS OUR FOUNDATION?

So will I break down the wall that ye have daubed with untempered mortar, and bring it down to the ground, so that the foundation thereof shall be discovered. - Ezekiel 13:14

In the above passage, the Lord is talking to Ezekiel about the lying prophets. But while I was reading it, one phrase jumped out at me: *so that the foundation thereof shall be discovered.* That phrase alone seemed to answer a lot of the questions I have been asking.

It has been a rough few months. Between job loss, car accidents (yes, that's plural), home repairs, etc., life has been very discouraging. I keep telling myself that God has it all under control and that He has our best interest at heart. But as soon as my spirit lifts a little, something else goes wrong and throws me right back down. I feel like I'm losing the strength and courage to even get back up.

I've cried to the Lord. I've wondered if this was a trial from the devil or simply the Lord trying to get my attention to lead me in a new direction. I'm still not completely sure which it is. But that phrase seemed to speak to me. I may not know where the trouble is coming from, but I think I know why it is coming. I'm being tested so that my foundation might be discovered. How firm is my foundation? Am I truly standing on the Solid Rock?

I'm not doubting my salvation, mind you. I'm saved, and I know it. The question is not have I trusted in Jesus to save me, but am I trusting Him daily with the events of my life. When the money is gone, the job is lost, the cars are wrecked, and the house is falling apart, what's left? What do others see? Do they see a weak faith and a crushed spirit? Or do they see a weary Christian singing praises to the Lord through the tears? How firm is my foundation? Unfortunately, it's not as firm as it should be. Maybe, that's why the testing is still going on. Maybe God is waiting for me to pass the test. (I always did hate tests!)

I don't have all the answers, but I know Someone who does. All I can do is trust in Him to see me through. After all, He's the only One who can!

LIFE IS LIKE A GOOD STORY

Yesterday, I was tutoring a student in creative writing. This was our first real lesson, so I was explaining to her some things that every story must have. For example, a good story must have characters, a plot, a setting, a theme, etc. That part is easy. Almost everyone knows that. But, then I had to explain to her the first thing I learned when I studied creative writing.

A good story must have a problem or conflict. It sounds strange, I know, but think about every good book you've ever read. The story revolved around a problem or conflict. It wouldn't be much of a story if all was smooth sailing for your characters. In fact, it would be quite boring.

On the heels of this revelation, I had to explain why the story needs conflict. The answer is so that the main character can experience growth. The character at the end of the story should be a little different than the one at the beginning. Perhaps he is a little wiser or has a different attitude. Whatever the situation, character growth is essential to a good story.

Isn't life very similar? After all, God is writing our life stories. We are His main characters. Life itself is the plot. The time and place in which we exist are the setting. The theme is to honor Him and bring glory to Him. And the conflict? Well, we see those all the time. Don't we? Lost jobs, broken families, financial crises, etc. Yes, our story has plenty of conflict, but why?

So that we (the characters) can experience growth! The reason God allows us to go through trials is to help us grow into better Christians. How many times have we come out of a bad situation and found that we were better because of it? God is not punishing us by sending hard times. He's simply giving us a reason to improve. He is writing the ultimate story!

All scripture is given by inspiration of God, and is profitable for doctrine, for reproof, for correction, for instruction in righteousness: That the man of God may be perfect, throughly furnished unto all good works. - II Timothy 3:16-17

I SPY WITH MY LITTLE EYES

On Sunday mornings, while the adults are enjoying the preaching, we have a Junior Church for kids ages 4-11. A couple of our college-age girls teach this class.

On this particular Sunday, they were teaching about creation. To help make the point of how miraculous creation is, one of the girls used the following illustration. "You know how when Mom makes cookies, she gets out all the ingredients, mixes them together, and then you have cookies? Well, creation was even greater because God didn't even have any ingredients. He just spoke and the world was created." It was a very good example, I thought.

At the end of the lesson, she was asking questions to make sure everyone understood the lesson. Trying to be fair and making sure that all the children had a chance to answer a question, she turned to one of the youngest and asked, "So what did God make the world out of?" With a big grin, he shouted, "Cookies!"

The story is hilarious and typical of a young child, but sometimes I think we, like the four-year-old, fail to truly understand the magnificence of the world around us. Creation is a miracle! Life is a miracle! Look at the colors that surround us. The textures. The shapes and sizes. Listen to the sound of the birds, the bugs, or even the wind. We live in a beautiful world, and even though it isn't made of cookies (wouldn't that be a danger to my waistline), we ought to be thankful for it and express that thanks daily.

He hath made every thing beautiful in his time: also he hath set the world in their heart, so that no man can find out the work that God maketh from the beginning to the end. - Ecclesiastes 3:11

THE CART BEFORE THE HORSE

Matthew 6:25-34

Therefore I say unto you, Take no thought for your life, what ye shall eat, or what ye shall drink; nor yet for your body, what ye shall put on. Is not the life more than meat, and the body than raiment? Behold the fowls of the air: for they sow not, neither do they reap, nor gather into barns; yet your heavenly Father feedeth them. Are ye not much better than they? Which of you by taking thought can add one cubit unto his stature? And why take ye thought for raiment? Consider the lilies of the field, how they grow; they toil not, neither do they spin: And yet I say unto you, That even Solomon in all his glory was not arrayed like one of these. Wherefore, if God so clothe the grass of the field, which to day is, and to morrow is cast into the oven, shall he not much more clothe you, O ye of little faith? Therefore take no thought, saying, What shall we eat? or, What shall we drink? or, Wherewithal shall we be clothed? (For after all these things do the Gentiles seek:) for your heavenly Father knoweth that ye have need of all these things. But seek ye first the kingdom of God, and his righteousness; and all these things shall be added unto you. Take therefore no thought for the morrow: for the morrow shall take thought for the things of itself. Sufficient unto the day is the evil thereof.

There is a lot of good meat in these verses, but I want to focus on verse 33. It is probably the most well-known verse in this passage, but sometimes I think a few things get overlooked. Let's look at it again:

But seek ye first the kingdom of God, and his righteousness; and all these things shall be added unto you.

What things shall be added? If you go back to verse 25 and read up to verse 33, you'll find out. What things? All of the things that we are worried about! What are we going to eat? What are we going to wear? How are we going to pay the bills? These are all important questions, but more than that, they are questions that can cause us to lose our focus.

This verse tells us that if we will keep our priorities straight (i.e., focus on accomplishing God's will), God will meet all our needs. Maybe not all our wants, but definitely all our needs.

But when faced with so many questions and uncertainties, it's so easy to get distracted. It's so tempting to start scheming and plotting to find "the answers." The funny thing is that we already know the answer. It's right in front of us. We just fail to do it. Why? Honestly, because sometimes it's not as easy as it sounds, but that's not a very good excuse. Is it?

So, as we face the questions and problems of today, let's try to "seek first the kingdom of God." Then everything else will fall into place. It may not happen overnight, but it will happen. We have God's Word on it!

PLAYING THE SECOND FIDDLE

Yesterday I came across a quote that read, *It needs more skill than I can tell to play the second fiddle well.* I found this very interesting.

I love music. For upbeat, work music, I listen to Southern Gospel. But, during those times when I need to relax, I love listening to instrumental music. Two of my favorite pieces begin with a piano. The music is simple, yet lovely. However, in the middle of the song, the solemn tones of a cello appear. This combination usually moves me to tears. The two instruments are playing two different melodies, but they sound so beautiful together.

What amazes me is that when you look at the album cover, the name of the pianist (the one playing the MAIN instrument) is bold and prominent. However, the name of the cellist (the one playing the "second fiddle") is difficult to find. The song would have so little of its beauty without the second instrument, yet little recognition is given to the one who added such harmony to the music.

In following the Lord's leadership, we often find ourselves completing tasks that add beauty or harmony to someone else's work and receiving little credit in return. On the surface, this seems so unfair, but if you think about it, it makes sense. If we are really doing things for Jesus (the MAIN musician), we won't want the praise and recognition. After all, what are our efforts compared to the Master's?

Sometimes, we need to remember that life is not about us. It's about doing all things for the glory of the Lord. If that seems difficult (and I know it sometimes does), then just remember this. Jesus knows what we're doing, and He will reward us for our efforts. Isn't that all the recognition we need?

So, go on. Make some beautiful music today and give all the honor and glory to the Lord. He deserves it!

And whatsoever ye do, do it heartily, as to the Lord, and not unto men. - Colossians 3:23

DO YOUR ROOTS RUN DEEP?

My husband and I just got back from doing some yard work over at my sister's house. She had asked us about using Jason's '79 Bronco (nicknamed "The Beast") to pull up some stumps and small trees. We knew The Beast was equal to the task, so we headed over to her house just before lunch.

Three of the four trees/stumps came up out of the ground with no problem. The fourth, however, seemed to have a mind of its own, and it was determined that it was staying put. Even The Beast, with all its strength and power, could not pull that tree from the ground. We ended up ripping the tree into smaller pieces and breaking it off nearly level with the ground. That was all we could do. The tree wouldn't budge.

It caused me to think about how strong the roots must be and how firmly the tree was planted in the earth. This, in turn, made me examine my spiritual roots. Are they strong enough to weather adversity? Do I have a deep-rooted faith? Or, am I like the other three trees that simply surrendered when things got tough?

How about you? How are your roots today? If adversity should strike, are you firmly grounded in your faith? It's a tough question. Isn't it?

But without faith it is impossible to please him. – Hebrews 11:6

PARACHUTES AND LIFE JACKETS

We've all heard the phrase "leaning on Jesus." No doubt, we've said or sung it at some point in our lives. But have we ever stopped to think about what it really means to lean on Jesus? Let's try this little experiment.

Go lean on the wall. I mean, really lean on it. Put all your weight on the wall. Now, imagine that someone pulled that wall out from under you. Would you fall? If you truly had all your weight on the wall, yes, you would fall. However, what many of us consider "leaning" is not really leaning at all. We set up "safety nets" to ensure that if anything happens, we won't fall. Those safety nets come in all shapes and sizes, but we all have them. Sometimes it's our jobs. Sometimes it's our families or friends. Sometimes we find it in places we would never expect.

Now, that being said, do we really lean on Jesus or do we have safety nets all around for the times that things don't go the way we think they should? Peter leaned on Jesus when he walked on the water. He stepped out onto the waves and away from the boat, trusting that Jesus would keep him safe. Do we do the same or are we reaching out to Jesus with one hand while clutching the boat with the other? Listen to how Pastor Ron Mehl puts it:

You aren't truly trusting until you're slightly out of control--like Peter when he stepped out on the water. You aren't truly trusting until you've leaned so hard on Him that if you fell, you couldn't catch yourself. Trust means setting aside all secondary options, backup systems, and emergency parachutes. Trust says, "I've gone so far now that there's no return for me. If God doesn't save me and hold me up, I'll go under."
-What God Whispers in the Night

Oh, that we could all have faith such as that. Let that be our prayer today!

Trust in the LORD with all thine heart; and lean not unto thine own understanding. - Proverbs 3:5

DO YOU NEED SPIRITUAL FUEL?

Gas prices. It seems like that's all some people can talk about. You turn on the news, and you hear about gas prices. You pick up the paper, and you read about gas prices. Frankly, I'm tired of hearing about it. Does the constant rise in gas prices affect me? Of course. Am I aggravated that it takes more money to feed my car than it does to feed my family? Absolutely.

But how does complaining about it help any of us? How does it help to keep such a negative topic in the forefront of our minds day after day? It doesn't help us at all. In fact, it hinders us from focusing on more important things, like spiritual fuel.

I don't know a lot about cars (in fact, I know less about cars than I do about plants), but I do know that they must have gas before they will run. No fuel, no go! Our bodies work in the same way. God created us in such a way that our bodies need nourishment from food in order to work properly. So, acknowledging what we know about our physical bodies needing fuel, why should we think our spiritual bodies are any different? Why do we often deprive our faith of the fuel it needs to grow and thrive?

In Philippians 3, Paul said, *Brethren, I count not myself to have apprehended.* In other words, he's saying, "I've not arrived. I still have a lot of work to do on my faith." I think we can all say "Amen" to Paul's statement. I believe we can agree that we have not reached the level of spiritual maturity that we long for. We possess the faith, but are we fueling that faith?

The Bible compares the Christian walk with a race. So, let me ask you this question: how often are you making pit stops? I don't watch much auto racing, but more than once, I've seen a driver lose the race because his car ran out of gas. You can almost hear the conversation he has with himself as he passes that last pit stop. "I can make it a little farther. I have enough fuel to finish. If I just keep going, I'll win this thing."

Good thought. Bad plan. By not giving his car what it needed, he cost himself the race. Not only did he not win, but he didn't even get to finish.

Aren't we like that sometimes, too? So busy with our daily demands and weekly routines, we bypass our spiritual fuel. We know we need to read the Bible, but it's often just too difficult to fit it into our schedules. Our daily time with the Lord is interrupted by phone calls, sick children, or job emergencies. Day after day, we struggle through, forsaking our spiritual fuel, then wonder why life is so difficult and why we can't seem to gain any ground in our spiritual walk.

God has shown me time and time again that if I will devote the time to fueling my spiritual man, He will give me the time and energy to accomplish everything else on my "to do" list. Try it out. See what happens when your spiritual tank is full. It will cost you some time, but you'll soon discover that it's well worth the price.

WOLVES IN SHEEP'S CLOTHING

A funny thing happened this morning. My husband was fixing breakfast while I was taking care of a few other things around the house. I know he is VERY capable in the kitchen (much more so than I am), so I was a little surprised when I heard him groan in frustration.

When I looked in the frying pan, I realized immediately what the problem was. Instead of a pan full of hashbrowns, there was a pan full of french fries. I couldn't help but laugh. In his defense, the packages do look very similar, but the thought of french fries for breakfast was so hilarious to me. However, the more I thought about it, the more I realized that we are all guilty of doing the same thing. No, not cooking french fries instead of hashbrowns, but in not paying attention to the things that are important.

We live in a day filled with controversy and lies. The devil is hard at work, trying to make us doubt the Bible. False teachers surround us daily, filling us with their cynicism and hatred of all things true. We have to be careful because it's easy to get pulled in without even realizing it.

Here's an example. I was doing some research for another book that I'm writing when I came across a website called "Ex-Christians." Curious as I was, I clicked on it and started looking around. Wow! There are some really deceived people out there, and many of them are claiming to have "left Christianity."

It's time for us to pay attention. We need to be on the lookout for these false teachers and the deceitfulness of the devil. And the best way to determine a lie is to first know the truth. The truth can only be found in God's Word. If we know what it says, we'll be much better off in pointing out the lies around us. But we must pay attention. Otherwise, we may be facing a situation far worse than french fries for breakfast!

Beware of false prophets, which come to you in sheep's clothing, but inwardly they are ravening wolves. - Matthew 7:15

HIKES AND HEIGHTS

Yesterday, my husband and I decided to tackle the Natureland Trust Trail in Caesar's Head State Park. It is a 5.8-mile trail (one-way) that is rated "very strenuous." We had been on part of this trail months ago, and we were awed by its beauty. But that day, I was SO exhausted I feared making it out of the woods. (I can't remember how many times I told Jason, "Just leave me here. Save yourself.") Despite that, Jason has been wanting to go back and do the entire trail for a while now, but I've been afraid of it.

Yesterday, I faced my fear, and we walked/climbed the trail. It was tough! I have some terrible blisters, and my knees are sore. But that isn't what I wanted to tell you about it.

First of all, I want to say that if you desire more out of life, sometimes you have to get out of your comfort zone. Yesterday, I was WAY out of my comfort zone, but I had a great day!

Second, I want to tell you about The Cathedral. The Cathedral is a 120-foot semi-circular rock formation that you will find only on the Natureland Trust Trail. The trail is tucked up right against these rocks, so it's difficult to get a good picture. I don't think a picture could capture the "wow" of this place anyway (but that didn't keep us from trying).

As we stood there looking up, we each got a crick in the neck. It was so high. Most of the walls went straight up, but the section to the far left resembled the bottom side of a circular staircase. Because of all the recent rain, water was running down the rocks, causing a spray to hit us and refreshing us from the heat of the day. As we looked straight up, the drops appeared to be falling in slow motion. It was so awesome!

We stood there for several minutes trying to take it all in and searching for a word to describe it other than "awesome." We couldn't think of one. Then, as we were about to leave, I turned to Jason and said, "As awesome as this is, and as much as we can't take it in, how big is God? How awesome is He? How dumbstruck are we going to be when we see His face?" It's unimaginable! I think, even then, we'll be at a loss for words.

But as it is written, Eye hath not seen, nor ear heard, neither have entered into the heart of man, the things which God hath prepared for them that love him. - 1 Corinthians 2:9

NO QUESTIONS ASKED

Now upon the first day of the week, very early in the morning, they came unto the sepulchre, bringing the spices which they had prepared, and certain others with them. And they found the stone rolled away from the sepulchre. And they entered in, and found not the body of the Lord Jesus. - Luke 24:1-3

Yesterday morning, we were discussing the Resurrection in our ladies' Sunday School class. We read the different accounts of the Resurrection story and shared our feelings about certain verses or things that stood out to us.

One lady mentioned how special she thought it was that Jesus' first appearance was to a woman (and an adulterous woman at that). Another lady spoke of how the disciples didn't believe the women when they came and told that Jesus was alive and how often we are just as stubborn when it comes to having faith in things we don't understand. Many comments were made and opinions shared. However, we ran out of time before I was able to share something that came to my mind. So, I'll share it with you now.

In Luke 24, the Bible tells us that some women were going to the tomb of Jesus. They had spices with them which I believe they intended to use to help preserve the body of Christ. In short, they were on a mission.

My question is this: how did they intend to get to the body of Christ? Not only was it guarded by Roman soldiers, but there was a huge stone in front of the door. Did they think the soldiers would allow them to pass? Did they think that the soldiers would move the stone for them? Were the soldiers capable of moving a stone that size? Or were they doing what they were doing simply because they felt it was their duty? Is it possible that they gave no thought at all to how they were going to accomplish their mission? Is is possible that they were just that dedicated to their Savior?

We may never know the answers to those questions on this side of Heaven, but here's a question we can answer—are we dedicated enough to the Lord to do what we know He wants us to do without worrying about how we're going to do it? OUCH!!!!

Many times, we feel the Lord leading us to do something or to go down a certain path, but because we can't see all the answers, we fail to do His calling. He bids us to go to a foreign land, and we reply, "But I don't know the language." He calls us to teach, and we argue, "But I'm not good with people." He nudges us to make a donation, and we cry, "But I don't have enough to pay my own bills." We don't see the "how," so we fail to follow His commands.

We've all done it at least once, but are we still doing it? Or are we following the will of the Lord regardless of how many unanswered questions we have? The women with their spices were determined to fulfill their mission no matter what obstacles lay in their way. Are we willing to do the same? If so, think of the results. Their mission led them to the scene of a miracle. It's possible that ours may do the same, but we'll never find out if we aren't dedicated enough to try.

LIFE AND HIKING ARE SIMILAR

1. Sometimes the way is easy. Other times, it can be a struggle just to put one foot in front of the other.

2. There are many ups and downs

3. Sometimes the path is obvious and clearly marked. Other times, it can be difficult to find.

4. There are always obstacles to go over, under, around, or across.

5. You often meet travelers along the way who need a smile or a word of encouragement to carry on.

6. Sometimes you have to get out of your comfort zone and push yourself beyond what you think you're capable of.

7. Often you wonder if you'll ever make it to the end.

8. It's easier if you have someone traveling with you, pushing and encouraging.

9. Sometimes you feel too weary to go on.

10. In the end, you discover that the destination is worth it!

MULTIPLE CHOICE IS NOT ALWAYS EASIER

I despise making decisions. Often, when faced with a difficult decision, I envy the days of my youth when any choice could easily be made by the flawless "eeny, meeny, miny, mo" method. Such is not the case anymore.

Sometimes, I think I try so hard to make the right decision that I over-analyze and make things far more complicated than they should be. While it's important to me to follow the Lord's will, it is certainly not always easy to know what His will is. Some things are spelled out in the Bible. Thou shalt not kill, steal, lie, etc. It's there in black and white. Other things are not quite so obvious.

At times like this, it is imperative to listen intently for the still, small voice of God. Sounds easy, right? WRONG!!! Sometimes it's hard, and many times, it involves patience. (Yuck!) In fact, there have been times when I've tried so hard and waited so long for an answer that I've just given up and done whatever I thought was best. While it seemed like a good idea at the time, it ended in disaster. So why, at this moment, when faced with another decision and no sound from God, do I want to take matters into my own hands again? Haven't I learned my lesson? Somewhat. I haven't taken things into my hands . . . yet. I'm only thinking about it. That alone shows growth—small growth, but growth nonetheless. Oh, how I wish there were a Miracle-Gro for the Christian life!

So, what am I going to do? I'm going to try to wait. And while I'm waiting, I'll continue to listen. I guess, for right now, that's God's will for me.

Give ear to my prayer, O God; and hide not thyself from my supplication. - Psalm 55:1

NO LABELS REQUIRED

On my way home from running errands yesterday, I saw an unusual (and rather comical) sight. An old, beat-up truck was pulled over to the side of the road. A man, tools spread all around him, lay on the ground underneath the uncooperative vehicle. That's not the part that's unusual or comical. What was funny was that painted in large yellow letters on the tailgate of the truck was the word "CLUNKER." My first thought was, *No kidding!*

Don't get me wrong, I'm not belittling the fellow for having an old vehicle. Jason's bronco, The Beast, is almost as old as I am. It could appropriately be labeled as "CLUNKER," but don't tell Jason I said that. I understand that we have to make do with what we have. I just found it amusing that whoever painted that title on the vehicle felt that it was necessary. Anyone could look at truck and tell it was a clunker. No label was required.

The whole thing caused me to think about whether or not I need a label. When people look at me, is it obvious that I'm a Christian? Are my words, my actions, and my attitudes good representations of Christ? Am I living up to what God called me to be?

I've met many people who call themselves Christians, but I would have never made the connection. I can't judge their hearts, for only God knows whether or not they've trusted in Him. But I can see their attitudes and actions. I can hear their foul language. Their mean-spirited nature is evident. If not for their "Christian label," I would have pegged them as lost and on their way to Hell.

If we have to tell others that we are Christians, we're evidently not doing a very good job at representing Christ. Just as it was obvious that the old truck was a clunker, so should it be obvious that we are Christians. No labels should be necessary!

Now when they saw the boldness of Peter and John, and perceived that they were unlearned and ignorant men, they marvelled; and they took knowledge of them, that they had been with Jesus. - Acts 4:13

WHEN YOU DON'T HAVE A CLUE

Jason and I don't watch much television, but one of the few shows we really enjoy is *The Amazing Race*. In fact, we enjoy it so much that we watch the reruns online.

Recently, we were watching an episode, and I got really tickled at one of the teams. They were looking for the clue box on a bridge. (For those of you who aren't familiar with *The Amazing Race*, the clue box is a large box that sits on a tall red and yellow striped stand. It's pretty easy to spot.) Anyway, this couple walked right in front of the box several times saying, "Where is it? I just don't see it." Each time they walked past it, I had to laugh. It was so ridiculous. After a while, another team came and walked straight to the box. The first couple saw them, and one of them said, "Can you believe it? We walked right by it." The other replied, "No, I don't think it was there before." I laughed and laughed.

Later on, it hit me that I do the same thing that the couple did. I ask God for directions or instructions. He places them in an obvious place, and I walk right by them. "Where is it, Lord?"

"Where are my instructions?" I cringe to think that the angels in Heaven may be pointing down at me and laughing while saying, "Duh! It's right in front of you. You've walked past it five times!"

Needless to say, this has changed the way I watch *The Amazing Race*. Now, when people walk past a clue box and wander aimlessly, instead of laughing, I say a quick prayer that the Lord will help my eyes and ears to be open to all He is trying to convey to me. After all, I'm in a race, too, and I need to follow the instructions carefully if I'm going to reach the finish line.

Teach me thy way, O LORD, and lead me in a plain path, because of mine enemies. - Psalm 27:11

ARE YOU FINISHED YET?

At the end of the story of the Samaritan woman at the well, Jesus spoke these words, *My meat is to do the will of him that sent me, and to finish his work.*

Lately, Jason and I have been struggling with what direction the Lord wants us to go. Questions seem to surround us night and day. Things that were once clear are now hazy and uncertain. With all our hearts, we are striving to do the Lord's will, but many times I find myself asking, "Is it supposed to be this hard?"

When I read the passage in John about the Samaritan woman, that final verse struck a chord within me. It was then I experienced an "AHA" moment. Yes, we are trying to do the Lord's will, but have we finished doing the work that He has already led us to?

If you come to my house, the answer to that will be evident. You'll find unfinished projects every-where. The quilt I was going to mend. The bench Jason was building for my parents. The flower arrangement I told my mom I would fix for her. E-books that I was certain the Lord had intended for me to write. Articles that I've researched but never written. Book ideas that are now lost somewhere in my filing cabinet. And on and on the list could go.

It all boils down to this: God has given each of us a job to do, and until we've finished that job, He's not going to give us new instructions. For so long, I've been stuck on doing the Lord's will that I've forgotten to finish the Lord's will. (You'll find more on this topic in the chapter entitled *Distraction* in my book, *The Deadly Darts of the Devil*.)

It is VERY important to seek and do the Lord's will, but it's also important to finish the things we start. After all, that was Jesus' purpose when He was here on Earth, and think how bad things would be if He hadn't finished His work!

When Jesus therefore had received the vinegar, he said, It is finished: and he bowed his head, and gave up the ghost. - John 19:30

THE LOVE OF THE LORD

During the Easter season, I always feel my mind being pulled to another place. I imagine myself standing in the midst of an angry crowd. Above me, on a cruel wooden cross, hangs my Savior. If I hadn't seen Him being whipped and beaten, I wouldn't recognize the mutilated flesh displayed before me.

The sounds around me are a mixture of angry shouts and heartbroken sobs. Occasionally, even wicked laughter can be heard. The smell of blood is thick in the air, adding to the gorge that's already in my throat.

Sobs wrack my body and tears flow down my face as I watch my Lord struggle to draw in each breath, and with that breath ask His Father to forgive the ones that have put Him here. His marred face shows no anger, only love and compassion.

"Why?" I ask in anguish. "Why must You do this? Why must You suffer for sins that are not Your own?"

Jesus smiles down at me and answers, "So that you will never have to. For that, my child, is how much I love you."

He raises His head and utters a victorious cry, "IT IS FINISHED!" Then His eyes close, His head droops, and His breathing stills. My dearest Friend is dead.

But, this is not the end. . . .

For God so loved the world, that he gave his only begotten Son, that whosoever believeth in him should not perish, but have everlasting life. - John 3:16

OH, BE CAREFUL!

On a recent trip to Jones Gap State Park, Jason and I came upon a section of the park that had burned in a recent forest fire. Blackened tree branches lay twisted on the ground. Leaves that were once green and vibrant now hung limply, brown and decayed. Scorch marks stained the ground, providing even more evidence of the previous devastating event. The woods were quiet, and a great sadness hung in the air. What was once a beautiful place and a comforting home to many creatures was now nothing more than a depressing spot. And all because of someone's carelessness. Yes, the fire was started by a campfire that was not properly cared for. Carelessness created desolation.

As we wandered along the path, I began to think about how much pain and destruction can be caused by careless words and actions. Can you think of a time when you were hurt by someone saying or doing something careless? I'm sure we all can. Even more, I'm sure we can all think of a time when we said or did something careless and hurt someone else in the process.

We must be very careful. We need to think before we speak or act. We need to rein in our emotions. Carelessness on our part could lead to pain and devastation in the life of another.

The Bible has a lot to say about this topic. . . especially about the things that come out of our mouths. Check it out:

Even so the tongue is a little member, and boasteth great things. Behold, how great a matter a little fire kindleth! And the tongue is a fire, a world of iniquity: so is the tongue among our members, that it defileth the whole body, and setteth on fire the course of nature; and it is set on fire of hell. For every kind of beasts, and of birds, and of serpents, and of things in the sea, is tamed, and hath been tamed of mankind: But the tongue can no man tame; it is an unruly evil, full of deadly poison. - James 3:5-8

A word fitly spoken is like apples of gold in pictures of silver. - Proverbs 25:11

A soft answer turneth away wrath: but grievous words stir up anger. - Proverbs 15:1

For he that will love life, and see good days, let him refrain his tongue from evil, and his lips that they speak no guile. - 1 Peter 3:10

A good man out of the good treasure of his heart bringeth forth that which is good; and an evil man out of the evil treasure of his heart bringeth forth that which is evil: for of the abundance of the heart his mouth speaketh. - Luke 6:45

These verses and many more remind me of the children's song that I used to sing with my class when I taught kindergarten. It went like this, "Oh, be careful, little eyes, what you see; oh, be careful, little eyes, what you see, for the Father up above is looking down in love, so be careful, little eyes, what you see." The other verses state, "Oh, be careful, little ears, what you hear," "Oh, be careful, little mouth, what you say," "Oh, be careful, little hands, what you do," and "Oh, be careful, little feet, where you go." The song may be for children, but it's a lesson we would all do well to remember. Careless thoughts, words, and actions can cause a lot of damage, and just like the fire-damaged area, it may take a long time to repair the harm that was done.

FOCUS ON THE POSITIVE

Yesterday, the Lord allowed me to have a very effective Sunday School lesson. The funny thing is that I think I got more out of it than my teenage girls did, but maybe that's what the Lord intended.

I took a board game called "Visual Eyes." It contains numerous dice with different pictures on all sides. I told the girls they had a set amount of time to look at all of the dice and count all the animals. They worked frantically, making sure they looked at each of the dice and trying to remember the number in their heads. I called time, covered the dice with the box lid, and asked "Okay, how many sharp objects did you find?" Their faces fell. A couple looked confused. One spoke up, "That's not what you said to look for." "I know," I replied with a smile. "But I want to know how many sharp objects you found?" No one could tell me.

"Let's try this again," I said as I uncovered the box. "You have until the timer runs out to find out how many sharp items there are. Really pay attention this time." Again, they worked in a panic, trying to beat the clock and come up with the correct answer. When their time was up, I covered the dice again and asked, "How many articles of clothing did you find?" One girl screamed in frustration, then muttered "This is a stupid game." Once again, I couldn't find anyone to answer my question.

"Why can't you tell me?" I asked. "You just looked at the dice. In fact, you looked at them twice. Why can't you tell me what I want to know?" Several answered, "Because that's not what we were looking for." EXACTLY!

Then, I took them to Philippians 4:8 which says, *Finally, brethren, whatsoever things are true, whatsoever things are honest, whatsoever things are just, whatsoever things are pure, whatsoever things are lovely, whatsoever things are of good report; if there be any virtue, and if there be any praise, think on these things.*

If we're focused on the good things, it's hard to keep track of the bad. However, if we're focused on the bad things in our lives, it's difficult to see the good. Not only do we lose track of how many sharp objects there are on the dice, but we lose sight of all the blessings that God has given us.

These days, it's VERY easy to focus on the negative. Pick up a newspaper. Turn on the television. Listen to the conversations taking place around you. War. Economic crises. Job loss. Sickness. Disease. It's one bad thing after another, and frankly, it's easy to get pulled into the devil's trap of discouragement and depression. The really bad part is that while we're there, we forget all the good things in life. Salvation. Family. Friends. A loving church. Chocolate. Flowers. Chocolate. Sunshine. Chocolate. And I could go on and on. (Did I mention chocolate?)

The problem is focusing on the negative in our lives instead of the positive. So, what's the solution? I'm glad you asked. Look at what I Thessalonians 5:18 has to say. *In every thing give thanks: for this is the will of God in Christ Jesus concerning you.*

I have heard this verse misread and misquoted so many times. It does not say "**For** every thing give thanks." It says, "**In** every thing give thanks." What's the difference? Well, my husband lost his job. Am I supposed to be thankful for that? No, that's silly! But because my husband lost his job, we have had a lot of time to spend together lately. In fact, I got to spend my entire birthday with my husband and my two dogs. We went to the lake and spent the day together as a family. That would not have been possible if my husband had not been laid off.

Do you see the difference? In each circumstance that life throws at you, find something to be thankful for. Your thankfulness will get your focus off of the negative and back on the positive where it belongs.

Now, how many times did I use the word "positive" in this devotion? What do you mean you don't know? You're supposed to be focusing on it!

A BOATLOAD OF BLESSINGS

And it came to pass, that, as the people pressed upon him to hear the word of God, he stood by the lake of Gennesaret, and saw two ships standing by the lake: but the fishermen were gone out of them, and were washing their nets. And he entered into one of the ships, which was Simon's, and prayed him that he would thrust out a little from the land. And he sat down, and taught the people out of the ship. Now when he had left speaking, he said unto Simon, Launch out into the deep, and let down your nets for a draught. And Simon answering said unto him, Master, we have toiled all the night, and have taken nothing: nevertheless at thy word I will let down the net. - Luke 5:1-5

I want you to picture this story through your mind's eye. Jesus, standing tall at the edge of a great body of water. People gathered all around him, hanging on his every word. Two empty boats bobbing up and down on the water's surface.

Now, look off to the side. A group of fishermen sit huddled together, scrubbing their nets (not that they needed cleaning--after all, they had remained empty all night). Take a close look at these men. Their eyes bespeak weariness. Their expressions portray disappointment. Their posture indicates defeat. They had labored all night and had absolutely nothing to show for it. There was no fruit for their labor. There was no evidence that they had been hard at work. There were no fish, which meant there was no money. After all, fishing was their job.

If you listen carefully, you can even hear their conversation. "What do you think went wrong?" asks one fisherman. "I don't know," answers another. "Maybe this isn't what the Lord called us to do after all." "What's the use?" cries a third fisherman. "It's just too hard, and it's not fair. We work just as hard as the other fishermen. Why do they get all the profits while we sit here with empty nets and heavy hearts?"

Have you ever found yourself in a similar situation? Whether it be your job, your family, your church, or something else entirely. You put your effort into it day after day only to be rewarded with pain and disappointment. You work hard, doing the tasks that you believe God has called you to do, and NOTHING! No fruit! No reward! No compensation! Nothing but the bitter taste of defeat. You feel like giving up. You feel like changing directions. You question if maybe you heard God wrong, and this is not His will after all. But most of all, you doubt. You doubt if

God even cares about you or what you're going through. Sound familiar? If so, read on.

And when they had this done, they inclosed a great multitude of fishes: and their net brake. And they beckoned unto their partners, which were in the other ship, that they should come and help them. And they came, and filled both the ships, so that they began to sink. When Simon Peter saw it, he fell down at Jesus' knees, saying, Depart from me; for I am a sinful man, O Lord. For he was astonished, and all that were with him at the draught of the fishes which they had taken. - Luke 5:6-9

Did you catch what just happened? The fishermen had toiled all night (the best time for fishing, mind you) and hadn't caught a thing. But now, in God's time, they caught so many fish that their nets broke and two boats started to sink under the weight. (Imagine the smell!)

God still works miracles today, but He does so in His own time, just as He has always done. His ways are not our ways. They may not make sense to us. They may not seem the best to us. But if we will allow Him to lead us and if we will be faithful to follow that leadership, we will see miracles. Our disappointment will be replaced with great joy. We will be able to trade our defeat for victory. But we must wait on God. It's difficult, I know, but miracles don't happen without Him.

If you're weighed down with questions today about God's purpose for you and your ministry, talk to God about it. Follow His leadership, and then wait for His miracle. It will come, but only in His time! And when it does come, it will take more than two boats to hold the blessings!

PROVISIONS, PROPHETS, PROMISES

And Elijah the Tishbite, who was of the inhabitants of Gilead, said unto Ahab, As the LORD God of Israel liveth, before whom I stand, there shall not be dew nor rain these years, but according to my word. And the word of the LORD came unto him, saying, Get thee hence, and turn thee eastward, and hide thyself by the brook Cherith, that is before Jordan. And it shall be, that thou shalt drink of the brook; and I have commanded the ravens to feed thee there. So he went and did according unto the word of the LORD: for he went and dwelt by the brook Cherith, that is before Jordan. And the ravens brought him bread and flesh in the morning, and bread and flesh in the evening; and he drank of the brook. And it came to pass after a while, that the brook dried up, because there had been no rain in the land. And the word of the LORD came unto him, saying, Arise, get thee to Zarephath, which belongeth to Zidon, and dwell there; behold, I have commanded a widow woman there to sustain thee. -- 1 Kings 17:1-9

There is some very important information in these few verses, and it can easily be missed. I know I didn't notice it until my pastor pointed it out a couple of weeks ago.

God commanded Elijah to go to the brook and wait for further instructions. But before Elijah left, God said *I have commanded the ravens to feed thee there.* Notice that — "I have commanded," not "I will command." God had already made provision for Elijah. Before the prophet even realized he had a need, God had met that need.

Now, if you'll notice, in verse 9, God commands Elijah to go to Zarephath. He tells the prophet, *I have commanded a widow woman there to sustain thee.* Did you catch it again? "I have commanded" means that it was already done. God knew what Elijah would be needing, and He met those needs.

I know that many people right now are going through difficult times. It seems like darkness is all around us and our prayers are going unheard. Don't despair. Just as with Elijah, God knows our needs, and He will meet those needs in His time. It's hard, and often, it's confusing, but we must have faith. God will pass by at the right time!

PINING FOR HOME

Life is never boring! At least, my life isn't. We had a major snow storm come through yesterday. It was like none I have ever seen before. This one was complete with heavy winds and eerie blue lightning. Spookular!

Jason and I were at my sister's house yesterday afternoon, just hanging out until church. Shortly after 5:00, the snow began to fall. By 5:30, it had already accumulated on the trees, grass, and roads. We called our pastor and asked about the evening service. He said he wasn't sure, so we agreed to meet him at the church since it was on our way home anyway.

We were the only ones who showed up. (Everyone else was smart!) By the time we left, which was only 20 minutes later, the ground was completely covered and the visibility was not good at all. Despite my better judgment, we went home the back way since we were in The Beast (the big, ugly 4x4 Bronco, which has NO heat, I might add).

We had not gotten far before we came upon two vehicles that were stuck and couldn't make it up the hill. We pulled one guy up while another truck stopped and helped the other. Shortly after that, we pulled into a gas station to make sure we had plenty of fuel and to clean off the windshield which was covered with icy snow.

Just a couple of miles further, we were going down a hill and noticed a long string of oncoming traffic that seemed to be stopped. The people in the lead car had heard the sound of a breaking tree. Unfortunately, we didn't. We did see it as it fell 15 feet in front of us, and then we saw it VERY closely as we slid into it. OUCH! Some people jumped out of their cars to make sure we were okay. We were fine, just shaken. The Beast, however, has a few minor injuries (like it wasn't ugly enough before).

Jason and some of the other men went to work cutting up the huge pine tree and dragging it off the road so that the endless line of traffic could pass. (Thankfully, Jason had his chainsaw with him.) I sat in the truck and shivered while they were about their work.

Red-faced and soaking wet, Jason got back in the abused Bronco, and we made it another mile or so before we ran into another line of traffic. This time I was on the lookout for falling trees. Whatever was blocking the road was a good half mile ahead of us, and from what we could gather, it was a utility pole. Assuming we would be there a while, we decided to turn back and see if we could go around it. Believe it or not, that actually worked. (Yeah, I'm surprised, too.)

We made our way home, peering through a foggy windshield that was again covered with icy snow. We inched through dark intersections, all the while praying that we would have power at our house. We did! (Another shocker!)

I honestly don't think I've ever been so glad to get home in my life. The trip from church to our house is a 30-minute drive. It took us an hour and a half last night. When we finally got home, I was so cold and so stiff, all I could do was stand in front of the wood stove and fight back the tears of thank-fulness.

You know, life is like that. Sometimes it seems so difficult just to get through. There are obstacles in the way, and often it's hard to even see where we're going. Many times, the trip is cold and frightening, and it seems that we'll never reach our destination.

Can you imagine how great our homecoming will be? Can you imagine the joy and relief at finally reaching our destination? Can you imagine the peace of knowing that we'll never have to face life's situations again?

I'm ready for that day. Are you?

His lord said unto him, Well done, thou good and faithful servant: thou hast been faithful over a few things, I will make thee ruler over many things: enter thou into the joy of thy lord. - Matthew 25:21

ONE SIZE DOES NOT FIT ALL

And Saul armed David with his armour, and he put an helmet of brass upon his head; also he armed him with a coat of mail. And David girded his sword upon his armour, and he assayed to go; for he had not proved it. And David said unto Saul, I cannot go with these; for I have not proved them. And David put them off him. And he took his staff in his hand, and chose him five smooth stones out of the brook, and put them in a shepherd's bag which he had, even in a scrip; and his sling was in his hand; and he drew near to the Philistine. – 1 Samuel 17:38-40

We all know the rest of the story. David faces Goliath and brings him face down in the dirt with a stone from his sling (not to mention a mighty shove from God). Have you ever wondered what would have happened if David had faced Goliath as Saul intended for him to do? What if David had gone out wearing over-sized armor and carrying a sword that was likely as big as he was? What would have been the outcome?

David was wise enough to know that one size does not fit all (despite what some clothing tags may say). What may have worked best for Saul was not necessarily what would work best for David.

That's an important lesson for each of us to remember.

Often in life, we try to get through by using someone else's strategy. We listen to advice from television talk show hosts and wonder why things in our lives aren't working out the way they should. We follow in the footsteps of our heroes, yet fail to accomplish even an inkling of what they've accomplished. This leaves us doubting our purpose in life and weary of going on, but could it be that we are trying to fight life's battles in someone else's armor?

God did not create all of us with the same talents or personalities. We are each unique. He has a distinct purpose and plan for each of us, and His will can only be performed by using the tools He has equipped us with.

Let me give you another example. When it comes to cars, I'm an idiot. I can put gas in the tank, and sometimes I can figure out how to get the hood open. That's about it. I don't know how to change the spark plugs or even charge the battery. My husband, on the other hand, can take engines apart and put them back together with minimal effort. When he talks "car talk" with me, it's like hearing Charlie Brown's teacher. "Wah, wah, wah, wah." He's using words, but they don't mean a thing to me.

So, of the two of us, which one would make a better mechanic? Obviously, the one who has the knowledge and the tools to perform the job.

That's how life is. We each have a purpose. It's our job to find out what it is and to do it. The best place to start in finding out what plans God has for us is to stop trying to use the tools of others and instead look at the tools He's given us. It's good to have role models, but just because something worked for them does not mean it will work for us. We must find God's specific will for our lives.

So, what tools do you possess? Patience? Skill with numbers? Love of animals? Musical talent? Gather your tools today and put them to work for the glory of God. After all, our paths will be much smoother if we'll stop lugging around over-sized armor and hand-and-a-half swords. Let's stick to our own tools...even if they're as simple as a sling and a stone.

DO YOU SEE GOD AT WORK?

We all know the story of Shadrach, Meshach, and Abednego. They were three Hebrew children who stood up for what they believed in and faced a fiery furnace as a result. I want you to read the following passage carefully:

And these three men, Shadrach, Meshach, and Abednego, fell down bound into the midst of the burning fiery furnace. Then Nebuchadnezzar the king was astonied, and rose up in haste, [and] spake, and said unto his counsellors, Did not we cast three men bound into the midst of the fire? They answered and said unto the king, True, O king. He answered and said, Lo, I see four men loose, walking in the midst of the fire, and they have no hurt; and the form of the fourth is like the Son of God. Then Nebuchadnezzar came near to the mouth of the burning fiery furnace, [and] spake, and said, Shadrach, Meshach, and Abednego, ye servants of the most high God, come forth, and come [hither]. Then Shadrach, Meshach, and Abednego, came forth of the midst of the fire. - Daniel 3:23-26

Did you see anywhere in that passage where the three Hebrew children saw God in the midst of their fiery trial? No? I didn't either. We know that Nebuchadnezzar could see God walking through the fire, but could Shadrach, Meshach, and Abednego? They knew God was with them because they believed in His promise that He would never leave them nor forsake them, but did they actually see Him walking with them in the midst of their trial? We may never know the answer until we get to Heaven, but I think there's a powerful lesson here.

Have you ever been through a trial where you felt you were all alone and no one cared? Have you ever struggled to see God in the midst of your troubles? Have you ever questioned if God is really working on your behalf? Honestly, I have.

For me, life is often filled with unanswered questions, doubts, worries, and fear. At times, I've even asked God why things had to be so difficult. I'm still waiting on that answer. But by thinking on this story of the three Hebrew children, I realize they must have felt the same way I do now. They stood up for what was right. They did what they knew to be right, and the next thing they knew they were being thrown into a literal "Hell on Earth." Though their faith was strong, I'm sure at some point they wondered why life had to be so hard and why God wasn't there to help them.

Although I feel I face many of life's fiery trials alone, I can have faith that God is with me. I can know that even though I may not see Him walking with me through the fire, He's still there. That's what faith is all about—believing without seeing. The real blessing comes in knowing that others will be able to see His presence in the grace, strength, and peace He gives me through the difficult times. Nebuchadnezzar and his entire kingdom were changed because of what he saw that day. When we allow God to work through our lives (even in the tough times), we can make a difference in the lives of those who witness His presence. Will you allow God to work through you today?

THE UGLY DUCKLING

And Laban had two daughters: the name of the elder was Leah, and the name of the younger was Rachel. Leah was tender eyed; but Rachel was beautiful and well favoured. - Genesis 29:16-17

Have you ever been the victim of rejection? Have you ever been a contestant in a game of favorites and lost? If anyone knew the pain of rejection, it was Leah. She was treated differently because she was not as attractive as her sister. Can you imagine how much Leah must have hurt knowing that she was not loved as much because of her looks? Rejection is painful!

Maybe you've never faced that kind of rejection. Perhaps your rejection is of a different sort. Could it be that you were fired from a job because "the other guy" was a suck-up? Maybe you've eaten your lunch alone because you weren't popular enough to eat with the "in crowd." Perhaps your loved one walked out on you because he found "someone better." At some point in our lives we have all faced rejection.

Right now, I have a folder in my filing cabinet labeled "Rejections." In the writing world, rejections are just a part of life. My folder is full of letters saying, "Thank you for sending us your manuscript. We regret that we cannot use it at this time. . ." It hurts. Every time I get one of those letters a little part of my excitement for writing dies. Rejection is painful!

The good news is that God knows all about our rejection. He knows how much we hurt. He knows all about our heavy hearts. He knows, and He cares. If you'll read on in chapter 29 of Genesis, you'll see how God dealt with Leah's rejection.

And when the Lord saw that Leah was hated, he opened her womb: but Rachel was barren. . .And she conceived again, and bare a son: and she said, Now will I praise the Lord: therefore she called his name Judah; and left bearing. - Genesis 29:31,35

Not only did the Lord give Leah children, He gave her Judah, the child who would be the start of the line of Christ. What a gift! True, Leah may have been rejected by her family and friends, but she was never rejected by God.

The same can be said of us. Many times it seems like we don't have a friend to stand with us. At times, we can be brought so low that we wonder if anyone really cares. Well, I'm here to remind each of us that God does care. He will never reject us! After all, we were ugly in our trespasses and sin, yet He still sent His only Son to die for us. Now that's acceptance!

DON'T WORRY, BE HAPPY

Last week, Jason and I took our two dogs back to Lake Wattacoo. Since there was no one there and the trail is not located in a state park, we decided to give them a little freedom. We took off their leashes and allowed them to travel at their own pace.

Mitch, always so full of energy, would run ahead for a little ways and then run back to us. He would run up the sloping sides of the trail, through the woods, then cross to the other side and do the same thing.

Tippy, who is a little overweight and a good bit older than Mitch, lagged behind at her own pace, stopping every now and then to sniff and mark. Still, she made an effort to keep up, which is more than she'll do when she's on the leash. (She has a bit of a stubborn streak. I think I know someone else like that.)

We walked the trail until we reached the lake, then we decided to see if they would run and play, yet stay within our sight. So, Jason and I sat down on the ground in front of the lake and just spent some time enjoying one another's company. Before long, the dogs had wandered off, exploring every nook and cranny (and mud hole). We spent probably close to thirty minutes just sitting at the lake and allowing the dogs to run free. They loved it!

On our way back up the trail, Mitch decided he wanted to play tag, so he'd run ahead, then circle back and tag one of us when we weren't looking. (Tippy was not thrilled about this game.) He ran and played and looked so happy with his wide tongue hanging out of the side of his mouth. I laughed at him until my face was literally hurting. Jason turned to me and asked, "What's so funny?' With a huge grin, I said, "I'm just happy to see him so happy."

That thought has stuck with me for several days now. For those of you with children, doesn't it make you happy to see your children happy? For me, my dogs are my children, so I can't help but smile when I know they're enjoying life. Do you think our Heavenly Father is any different? Don't you suppose it makes Him happy to see us happy? I think so. I think He smiles when we smile and laughs when we laugh. I think He's blessed when He sees us enjoying life.

So what about the hard times? What about those times when life is not so enjoyable? During those times, He knows our pain, and if we can still smile through our tears, He smiles that much more. It's like the song Rodney Griffin wrote, "God Wants to Hear You Sing." God's happy when we smile during the good times, but He's really pleased when we can still smile through the bad times.

Make God happy today—be happy!

Delight thyself also in the LORD; and he shall give thee the desires of thine heart. - Psalm 37:4

SAFETY IN THE SHADOW

He that dwelleth in the secret place of the most High shall abide under the shadow of the Almighty. - Psalm 91:1

Over and over again, the Scriptures speak of being in the shadow of the Almighty or in the shadow of His wings. So, what does that mean exactly? It means to be close—very close!

Let's try this little experiment. (If it happens to be raining or cloudy the day you're reading this, you will want to wait until later.) Go outside and look around. Find some shadows that are being cast by trees, buildings, vehicles, etc. Now, go stand in those shadows. How close did you have to get to each object to abide in its shadow? Pretty close, huh? The same is true with God.

There is no safer place than in the shadow of the Almighty, but many times we aren't close enough to Him to know the peace and joy that come from such safety.

Some of you are probably thinking, *But God is big and therefore must cast a huge shadow. Plus, He is everywhere; therefore, His shadow would be everywhere too.* Those are good points, but bear with me. I'm trying to make a different point here.

In order to stand in the shadow of an object, you must be close to it. If we're not in God's shadow, that means we're not close enough. If we're not close enough to God, we have some problems that we need to get settled. After all, our intimacy with God is determined by us. God is providing a shadow, and if we're not in it, that's our fault.

This topic always makes me think of how chickens and other birds react when a storm comes. The mother bird does not run around trying to persuade each chick to run into the shelter of her wings. No, the little birds come running to her out of fear and instinct. All she has to do is stand there with her wings up, waiting for her children to run to safety.

God has gone so much farther than that. He sent His Son to die for our sins. He gave us His Book to guide us in our lives and to remind us daily of His love for us. He calls to us continually to run and hide under His wings, but in our pride and stubbornness, we do not heed His call. We try to do things on our own and wind up in a huge mess. Why, oh, why do we do that?

Today, God is waiting for you. His wing is extended, and His shadow cast. Whether or not you abide there is up to you. Come on. Step into His shadow!

WHO'S THE BOSS?

In the midst of dark times, it's easy to forget that God is in control. It seems as if God has forsaken us and left us to work things out for ourselves. But, we know that is not the case. I can't explain why God does some of the things He does, but I do know that He knows best.

I was thinking about these things during my Bible reading this morning, and three little words jumped out. These three words are so simple, but they can bring such peace. One simple phrase reminds us that God is still on the throne, and no matter how dire the circumstances around us are, His plan will be fulfilled.

Yea, before the day was I am he; and there is none that can deliver out of my hand: I will work, and who shall let it? - Isaiah 43:13

In this passage, God is speaking. I realize that He is talking to Israel, but I think the message applies to us just the same. God says, "I will work." No "ifs," "ands," or "buts." God will work. In fact, He is working right now. He is doing something wonderful for His children, and our job is to follow His leadership and then sit back in faith and watch things unfold.

Things may get worse before they get better, but God knows that. He has seen the beginning and the end. None of this is a surprise to Him. He's not sitting up in Heaven wringing His hands and wondering how He's going to make it all work. He has a plan, and He will see it fulfilled. Period! Isn't that a cause for celebration?

EXTRA BAGGAGE

Last Saturday we took our dogs over to Chestnut Ridge, a heritage preserve about 20 minutes from our house. The 2.5 mile trail is a moderate, but beautiful hike down to the peace and serenity of a gently flowing stream. It's one of our favorite places to go.

When we arrived at the gate to the heritage preserve, we stopped the truck and got out. The dogs immediately started running to and fro, exploring and looking for a place to go to the bathroom. We allow them this freedom because they know not to get out of our sight, and they're very well-behaved.

While Jason and I were getting our gear together, Mitch found an interesting item that he wanted to explore more closely. By the time Jason and I noticed what he had gotten into, it was too late. He had found the skeleton of a rather large animal and decided to roll in it. (Why do dogs do that?) As soon as Jason realized what Mitch was doing, he called him to come back to the truck. Mitch stood up and ran over to us but was immediately spooked by something that had hold of his collar. Fear filled his eyes as he ran faster towards us, a large white blur hanging from his collar and bouncing from side to side as he ran. Once we got him stopped, we discovered the item to be the backbone of the skeleton he had rolled in. GROSS!!!! When Mitch had rolled on the ground, part of the backbone had gotten tangled in his collar. Jason had to work it loose and dispose of it. (I certainly wasn't going to touch it!!!)

Mitch didn't know what to think. To him, he was just doing a little exploring, but he got much more than what he had planned on. Not only had he been "grabbed" by a dead animal but at that point he smelled like one too. He wasn't pleased. After I had calmed him down, I patted him on the head and said, "That's what happens when you get into stuff that you're not supposed to mess with." WHACK! God thumped me right between the eyes.

Many times in life, we have a knack for getting ourselves into difficult situations. Why? Just like Mitch, we do things we know we're not supposed to do. We go where we shouldn't go, watch what we shouldn't watch, listen to things better left unheard, and say things better left unsaid. We get into things that we have no business messing with and then wonder why things are going wrong in our lives. Just as Mitch got more than he had planned on, so do we when we do the wrong things. Remember the old song, "Sin Will Take You Farther Than You Want to Go"? It's true. We would be much better off if we would stick to the right path and not wander off to go "exploring." After all, who wants to carry around all that extra baggage (especially if it's part of a skeleton)?

Keep thy heart with all diligence; for out of it are the issues of life.
- Proverbs 4:23

REPETITION AIDS LEARNING

Have you ever noticed how God has a way of getting a point across in the Bible? Sometimes, it's almost comical how He beats people over the head in order to get their attention or to make a point. (I have also been the recipient of that head-beating, and it's not so comical then.) Anyway, in my Bible reading, I found another occasion where God was trying to make a point.

Oh that men would praise the Lord for his goodness, and for his wonderful works to the children of men! - Psalm 107: 8, 15, 21, 31.

Did you catch that? Those four verses read exactly the same. God put the same sentence in this one psalm four times. Why? Could it be that He wanted to make sure we didn't miss it. After all, it's a very important verse. Through this passage, the psalmist is talking about how God provided for the children of Israel and delivered them from Egypt. Yet they were not happy. They complained of hunger, thirst, fatigue, obstacles. You name it, they complained about it.

So, the story is being told. They complained, and God said, *Oh that men would praise the Lord.*

They rebelled, and God said, *Oh that men would praise the Lord*. They cried, and God said, *Oh that men would praise the Lord*. They worshipped idols, and God said, *Oh that men would praise the Lord*. Do we get the point?

The Israelites were so wrapped up in their complaints and criticism that they ignored or forgot (I often wonder which) all the things that God did for them. He fed them with manna and quail. He gave them water from the rock. He delivered them from captivity. Their clothes never wore out. He continuously forgave them for their bickering and sinful acts. But did they appreciate it? No, they complained!

Now, before we get too hard on the children of Israel, aren't we often the same way? When tragedy or hardships come, don't we often fret and forget how God delivered us in the past? We focus on our problems instead of on the solution. We complain about our current state and wonder why life is so unfair.

This psalm is an excellent reminder to all of us that no matter what we face, good or bad, we need to praise the Lord. He has been good, and

He has done wonderful works. Shame on us for overlooking that!

Whatever you're facing today, put aside the complaints and murmurs, and instead praise the Lord for all that He's done. After that, the problem may not look so bad anymore.

LIGHT AT THE END OF THE TUNNEL

The verses that I spoke of in the last devotion, "Repetition Aids Learning," really fascinated me. In fact, I was so entranced by those verses that I completely missed some other powerful repetitions. Months after I wrote the last devotion, God brought these verses to my attention:

Vs. 6 - Then they cried unto the LORD in their trouble, and he delivered them out of their distresses.

Vs. 13 - Then they cried unto the LORD in their trouble, and he saved them out of their distresses.

Vs. 19 - Then they cry unto the LORD in their trouble, and he saveth them out of their distresses.

Vs. 28 - Then they cry unto the LORD in their trouble, and he bringeth them out of their distresses.

This one passage tells us four times that the Lord delivered His people out of their distresses. You may be wondering what that has to do with us today. Do you realize that "distress" is a synonym for "stress"? Are any of you acquainted with stress? I think if we're honest, we would all agree that life can be very stressful. Living from paycheck to paycheck. Wondering if we'll still have a job tomorrow. Staring into the face of terrorism. Fearing what will become of our great country. Let's face it, life is stressful. But, here's the good news: God can deliver us out of that stress. How? I'm glad you asked.

1. He leads us in the way we need to go. - vs. 7
If we are faithful to follow the Lord's leading, we will stay in His will. If we are in His will, then all will be well. Does that mean no bad things will happen? No, but it means we will have peace knowing that we are where God wants us to be.

2. He brightens our days. - vs. 14
Ever feel like you're surrounded by darkness? Ever feel like there's no light to be found? I do, but the truth is Jesus is the Light. He can brighten even our darkest days if we'll allow Him to. Spend a few minutes with Him and see if you don't notice a ray of light on the horizon.

3. He speaks to us. - vs. 20
What a privilege to know that the God of this world takes time to speak to His children! He has given us His Word as a lamp for our feet and a

light for our path. He speaks to us through messages and songs. He nudges our hearts and whispers to us in His still, small voice. God still speaks. The question is, "Are we listening?"

4. *He calms our storms or our souls.* - vs. *29* The McKameys sing a song entitled "Sometimes He Calms Me." The message of the song is that sometimes it is God's will for us to go through a storm, but during those times in which He will not calm the storm, He can calm us. He gives us sweet peace to make it through the trial. He knows what we need, and as much as we don't like it, sometimes we need the storms. But even during those times, we need not to stress, for God can calm our troubled hearts.

One more thing. Did you notice that before God delivered Israel from their distress, they cried to Him? Yes, God knows our problems, but He still wants us to talk to Him. Spend some time with Him today and pour out your burdens to Him. Cry on His shoulder. Then allow His peace to settle over you and trust Him to bring you out of your distress.

FOCUSING ON DEAD TREES

While hiking on Paris Mountain, Jason and I came to an open cliff that overlooked the countryside. Stretched out before us lay a valley of towering pines and mighty oaks, hemlock and rhododendron. In the distance, we could see buildings of different shapes and sizes, hazy, but still visible.

But as we surveyed the beautiful scene, we were shocked to realize that we were both focused on the same sight—one dead tree in the midst of the many living. It wasn't a large tree. In fact, compared to many of the trees, it seemed small and insignificant. But for some reason, as we scanned our surroundings, that one dead tree caught our attention.

Isn't that the way it is with hard times in our lives? Most of the time, we're surrounded by good things—a beautiful scene. But when those trials arise, it seems like that's all we can focus on. They stand out in our lives just like that one dead tree stood out in the midst of the living. During these times, it's hard to see anything else, for no matter how hard we try, our attention keeps returning to the trial. It was for these times that God gave us Psalm 121.

I will lift up mine eyes unto the hills, from whence cometh my help. My help cometh from the LORD, which made heaven and earth. He will not suffer thy foot to be moved: he that keepeth thee will not slumber. Behold, he that keepeth Israel shall neither slumber nor sleep. The LORD is thy keeper: the LORD is thy shade upon thy right hand. The sun shall not smite thee by day, nor the moon by night. The LORD shall preserve thee from all evil: he shall preserve thy soul. The LORD shall preserve thy going out and thy coming in from this time forth, and even for evermore.

FIGHT OR FLIGHT?

A thought struck me from out of the blue yesterday. I have no idea where it came from, but it raised some interesting questions, and I've not been able to stop thinking about it.

We all know the story of Saul's jealousy of David and how Saul chased him and tried to kill him. My question is this: when David knew that Saul was angry with him, did he really need to run? After all, God had promised David that he would be king. So, Saul could not harm David, right? Was David's flight a lack of faith or just common sense?

This train of thought led me to wonder if it might have been God's will for David to stay put. How would things have been different? Would fewer people have been killed? Would David have earned such a faithful following?

I have no answers for this. If I were being chased, my first instinct would be to run, but our first instinct is not always God's will. Is it? I did not find anywhere in the Bible where the Lord told David to run. Interesting thought, isn't it?

ARE WE REALLY TOO BUSY?

I, for one, think life has become too hectic. It seems there is always something to do, somewhere to go, etc. Many times I feel like I don't have time to stop and catch my breath, but is that really the case?

I had a friend recently tell me that she didn't have time to do a particular thing, but later on in the conversation, she told me how she had spent several hours talking to people online. Which is it? After that, I noticed that several people around me were complaining about not having the time to do the things they want to do, yet again, in the same conversation they revealed countless time-wasters that they indulged in daily.

All of this made me wonder if I do the same thing. Do I complain about being busy when, in fact, I'm just wasting time? Now, don't get me wrong. We all need time to relax every now and then. That's not what I'm talking about. I'm talking about the hours spent on the cell phones, in front of the television, or at the computer. I'm talking about the numerous minutes that pass by without our awareness. Makes you think, doesn't it?

The moral of the story? I guess it would be to not complain about being too busy unless you can say without a doubt that you have not wasted any time. (That would stop a lot of complaining. Wouldn't it?)

Neither murmur ye, as some of them also murmured, and were destroyed of the destroyer. - 1 Corinthians 10:10

LITTLE IRRITATIONS

The piano at church has been driving me crazy. A few weeks ago while playing an offeratory, I noticed the high "A" key was sticking. It was annoying at the time, but I calmed myself by reminding myself that it wasn't a key I used often because I don't often play in the higher range.

About a week later, the "G" below middle "C" began sticking. It was far worse than the "A" and any of you who know about music know that that particular key is played ALL THE TIME! During one service, I was so distracted by the constant sticking that I wasn't paying attention to what I was doing. I stopped playing the hymn after the second verse, only to discover seconds later that there was another verse. The congregation was singing acapella because I was fiddling with the stuck note instead of playing the song. Needless to say, it was rather embarrassing.

Since that time, I have planned my offeratories around the stuck keys. It hasn't been easy, and I've had to remind myself to play that "G" an octave lower. I discovered that in trying to avoid those keys I messed up in other places. My "groove" was thrown off all because of a couple of stuck keys!

Do you see where I'm going with this? Many times in life, it only takes one wrong attitude or one bad habit to cause a major disruption in our Christian walk. These problems cause a note of discord in the beautiful melody God is trying to play through us. Whether it be a sin that we just won't let go of or an attitude of bitterness, these obstacles hinder us from making beautiful music for the Lord. Sure, we can "get by" just as I got by on the piano, but the melody won't sound as sweet. To restore the music, we need to fix the problems.

That's what made the difference with the church piano. The tuner/repairman came to look at the piano last week. He discovered the problem. Evidently, a mouse had decided to make his home inside the piano. He built himself a nest, chewed on some of the felt, and then died inside the piano. Why we didn't smell him I don't know! (Just think: I had been that close to a mouse for weeks and had no idea. Yuck!!!!) Anyway, the tuner removed the mouse (or what was left of him) and repaired the damage he had done. The piano plays perfectly now (although my groove could still use a little tweaking!)

What if we had ignored the problem and continued to try to "get by?" I cringe to think about it. There was a problem. It needed to be fixed. After the repairs were made, things were back as they should be.

God wants us to examine ourselves and see what belongs and what is out of place. A mouse in the piano is DEFINITELY out of place. How about your life? Do you see something that just doesn't belong? How about getting rid of it and allowing the Lord to use you again as an instrument for His glory!

Now that I know a mouse can get inside the piano, I'll be watching more carefully. I can't tell you the number of times I checked around my feet last Sunday. The same is true in our lives. Once we know what we're dealing with, we know what to watch out for. That will help us to keep pesky critters out of places they have no business being in.

Be sober, be vigilant; because your adversary the devil, as a roaring lion, walketh about, seeking whom he may devour. - 1 Peter 5:8

WHERE'S MY PILLAR?

It seems like a lot of things lately have revolved around seeking, finding, and obeying God's will. This theme has carried from my devotions to sermons, songs, and even my own Sunday School lesson. Somehow, the topic even came up in the car while Jason and I were out and about. Anytime, I see a theme running so rampantly through my life, I have to stop and ask, "Okay, God, what are You trying to tell me?"

I want SO MUCH to do the Lord's will, but honestly, sometimes I don't know if it's His voice I'm hearing or my own desires. Many times the Lord will practically have to beat me over the head with something before I'm convinced that it is His voice that I've been hearing. Jason and I often laugh over how difficult it is for God to convince me, but the truth is that I'm ashamed of my skepticism. After all, I should know His voice. Why can't I distinguish it from my own or from the myriad other noises that assault me day after day?

I'm reminded of the story of God leading the Israelites through the wilderness. You know the story, right? By day, they followed a cloud and by night, a pillar of fire. With such obvious symbols, the Israelites could be assured of two things: (1) God was in their midst; (2) they were heading in the right direction.

I don't have much trouble remembering that God is always with me. However, when it comes to knowing that I'm going in the right direction, I feel the need to ask for those pronounced symbols. I find myself asking God, "Why can't You lead me with a cloud or a pillar of fire? Why can't You make it that obvious for me?" When I receive His answer, I'll let you know what He says.

In the meantime, all I can do is study God's Word and keep a close relationship with Him in prayer. While the Bible may not tell us specifically whether to take a certain job or to invest in a certain business, it does give us vital information that we need each and every day. I've seen the Lord use a verse in the Scriptures to answer a very specific question, so I know that He will answer me when it is His time.

In addition, I must not forsake my precious prayer time. I need to remember that I'm there not only to talk, but also to listen. I need to work on tuning out the noise around me and focusing on God's voice so that I will recognize it when He speaks to me.

Would I rather have a cloud and a pillar of fire? Probably. But is that what would be best for me? Probably not. God has a way of helping us to grow, even when it's difficult and frustrating.

If you, like me, have trouble distinguishing God's voice, take heart. Read the Bible. Ask God for His direction. Then, listen to His answer and obey.

My sheep hear my voice, and I know them, and they follow me. - John 10:27

ANNUAL AMNESIA

Isn't it funny how many things we forget from one year to the next? I've been riding around for the past couple of weeks in complete awe of the beauty of autumn (maybe that should be spelled "awe"tumn). The colors are so vast and vibrant. The shades of red astound me, and that yellow-orange takes my breath away. I don't even know the names of many of the shades that are visible this time of year. Often, all I can say is "Ooh!" and "Aah!"

The amazing thing is that autumn is beautiful every year. Each year, we have the opportunity to study colors that only God could have thought of. We enjoy the crisp weather. We are fascinated by the colors. We can't wait to take that trip into the mountains. But come winter, all the joy of autumn is forgotten. How sad!

The Christian life can often be the same way. When we are on the mountain top, everything is beautiful. Life is good! We have our health. We have money in the bank. The road seems smooth. But as soon as hard times come, we instantly drop into despair and experience spiritual amnesia. We completely forget about the good times we've just had or the past troubles that God has seen us through. During these times, it seems like all we can do is focus on the problem at hand. We focus on the dark, cold winter.

Yes, winter can be tough, but it's necessary. Winter is a time of rest. It is a time for the plants and many of the animals to be renewed. Without winter, things just wouldn't work right. (Plus, we'd have no Christmas!)

Just as winter is necessary, hard times are also needed. It is during these times that we grow in our Christianity. It is during these times that we learn to trust God a little more. It is during these times that we realize how much God loves us. Painful? Sometimes. Necessary? Always.

My advice? First of all, if you haven't taken the time to enjoy the beauty outside your window, stop everything and go do it right now. I'm serious! Go take a deep breath of that invigorating air. Study the different shades around you and see if you can think of a name for each of them. (If you think of one for that shade that looks like red, orange, and yellow all blended together, let me know.) Above all, praise the God who loves us enough to surround us with such an awesome view.

Second, remember. Remember the good times and the bad. Remember that you will face hardships, but that beauty is waiting on the other side. Remember that God is faithful, and that He knows what you're going through. Remember that winter is only one season, and it too shall pass.

Now, if you'll excuse me, I have a date with my husband. We're going up to the mountains to do a little sight-seeing. After all, it's a beautiful day, and I don't want to waste it.

He hath made every thing beautiful in his time. - Ecclesiastes 3:11

'TIS THE SEASON

I love this time of year. I really do. The fall colors are beautiful. The cool air is refreshing. The holidays are full of joy and time spent with family. I love having the opportunity to celebrate the birth of Christ and a season to remember how much I have to be thankful for.

What I don't like about this time of year is how busy I become. Between Thanksgiving dinners, Christmas plays, programs, and presents, plus the various other obligations that come up this time of year, I find myself overwhelmed and not very much in the "holiday spirit." As of right now, I don't have all my food for Thanksgiving, I've only bought one Christmas present, and my December calendar is SCARY!

Could it be, like so many other things in our lives, we've complicated the joy right out of the holidays? If I'm not mistaken, the Christmas carol says, "Joy to the World" not "Stress to the World." We have to be very careful not to get so caught up in the holidays that we forget what they're truly about. They are supposed to be a time of remembrance, a time of praise, a time of thanksgiving, and a time of celebration. It's important that we not lose our focus (which is really easy to do when we're under so much stress). Let's be sure to keep this in mind as we jump from Christmas cantatas to gift shopping to cooking to wrapping to finding the perfect tree to . . .

Rejoice evermore. - 1 Thessalonians 5:16

THE GREATEST DEAL OF ALL TIME

Last Friday, millions of shoppers left their homes in the middle of the night in search of this year's greatest deals. Many stood out in the cold for hours as they waited for the shops to open. They braved the cold, the traffic, and the crowds in an effort to save money on their Christmas shopping.

I used to be one of those people, but not anymore. I have learned the joy of online shopping with free shipping, and I'll never go back to "the old way." Yes, while millions were freezing their bottoms off, I was sitting in bed reading a book. I was warm. I was comfortable. I was happy. For those who enjoy the thrill of the day, that's fine. I won't begrudge them that, but I prefer to stay in my warm bed.

I wonder, though, if sometimes we get so worked up about the latest and greatest deal that we forget the true "greatest" deal. What deal am I talking about? Salvation, of course. We didn't have to stand in line to get it. There wasn't a limited supply. We didn't have to get up early. We didn't have to fight the crowds. And best yet, we didn't even need a credit card. Salvation is a precious gift, and while it didn't cost us a thing, let us not forget that it cost Jesus His life. Yes, the greatest deal of all time was when we traded our filthy rags of sin for those holy white robes of atonement. We gave Jesus our guilt and shame, and in return He gave us a home in Heaven. That's a deal you won't find in the Black Friday ads!

For God so loved the world, that he gave his only begotten Son, that whosoever believeth in him should not perish, but have everlasting life. - John 3:16

THE GIFT OF GIVING

Yesterday, during my piano lessons, a couple of my students (who are brother and sister) reminded me of the joy of giving to others. I could tell when they arrived that they were excited about something, and it didn't take them long to tell me what had brought them such happiness. "We volunteered to help the Salvation Army make Christmas packages for needy families," they told me.

As they explained to me the process of choosing a needy family from the long list available at the Salvation Army, their eyes glowed with excitement. They went on to tell me how they basically get to shop for each member of the family and come up with a certain combination of outfits, toys, books, etc. The more my students spoke, the louder their voices became. By the end of their tale, they were literally bouncing off their chairs, barely able to contain their excitement. And all I could think was *Wow!*

We live in a day and age of such greed and selfishness. I've seen people get that excited about shopping for themselves but rarely for someone else. These children were absolutely thrilled to spend their time giving to someone else. How many of us can say the same?

I think the world would be a much better place if we could all find that joy of giving. After all, isn't that what this season is about? God gave His Son. Jesus gave His life. What have we given? It's something worth thinking about!

Every man according as he purposeth in his heart, so let him give; not grudgingly, or of necessity; for God loveth a cheerful giver. - II Corinthians 9:7

THE SOURCE OF MY SONG

Since the week of Christmas, I've been on Cloud Nine. I'm not sure why, but I've had such joy and peace for the past couple of weeks. That is, until yesterday. Yesterday, I fell off my cloud head first.

It's not that any one bad thing happened. It was just a bad day. I received three phone calls telling me that three different people I know were either sick or in the hospital. I worked for hours on a writing project that just would NOT come together. Then, to top it all off, I paid the bills. (Does anyone else get depressed while doing this?) I went to bed tired, tense, and frustrated.

In my prayer time this morning, I was pouring my heart out to the Lord. I told Him of my disappointment in not being on Cloud Nine anymore. I explained to Him how precious it was to have such peace, joy, and faith like I had had for the past couple of weeks. Then I said these words, "But I guess it had to end some time. After all, I can't always be on Cloud Nine."

No sooner had the words left my mouth that the Lord reminded me of a song by Rodney Griffin:

The source of my song is the Savior.
The reason for my singing is the Man from Galilee.
It does not depend upon my circumstances,
For Jesus is the source of my song.

I got the point! Who says we can't always be on Cloud Nine? If Jesus is truly the source of our song, bad days shouldn't get us down. Instead, they should remind us of how good God has been to us and make us aware of what He's trying to teach us.

I still don't feel the peace I had before, but today has been better than yesterday. And I know I can have that peace if I will keep focusing on Christ instead of the circumstances around me.

Finally, brethren, whatsoever things are true, whatsoever things are honest, whatsoever things are just, whatsoever things are pure, whatsoever things are lovely, whatsoever things are of good report; if there be any virtue, and if there be any praise, think on these things. - Philippians 4:8

WHERE ARE MY THREE WISHES?

As we pack away the Christmas decorations and Nativity scenes, let's not forget that every day is a reason to celebrate. Not only that, but let's be careful to not pack God away with the holiday stuff. What do I mean? As we settle back into our routines, it's easy to operate on autopilot and forget all about God. That is, until we need Him.

Have you ever thought about how much we use God? He gives us the rain we need, and we complain about ruined picnics. So, He gives us sunshine, and we fuss about the heat. He offers us blessing after blessing, and often we throw them back in His face. Some blessings we accept with gratitude, but many we grab without a second thought of where they come from. We neglect our daily time with God because, after all, we're very busy. We go to church out of duty or habit, not really seeking an opportunity to worship the Lord of Lords. But when trouble comes, boy, we're down on our knees in a hurry. Aren't we?

How sad! As this new year begins, one of my resolutions is to stop treating God like a spare tire or a genie in a bottle. Yes, He is a help in the time of need, but He is so much more! This year, I want my time with God to be special and precious. I want it to be more than me reciting a list of my wants and needs like a greedy child's Christmas list for Santa. I want to spend time with God as my Father, my Friend, and my Comforter. I want to stop using God and start treating Him with the love and respect He deserves.

I challenge you this year to focus some attention on your daily walk with God. As you enter into your special time with the Lord, don't forget about praise, worship, and thanksgiving. And remember to take some time just to bask in the presence of the Lord.

God loves each of us, but I'm sure He wearies of only being called upon to grant wishes. Let's not fall into this trap. It will take some time and effort on our part, but He is worth it!

What is it then? I will pray with the spirit, and I will pray with the understanding also: I will sing with the spirit, and I will sing with the understanding also. - 1 Corinthians 14:15

WALKING IN A WINNER'S WONDERLAND

I John 5:4 says, *For whatsoever is born of God overcometh the world: and this is the victory that overcometh the world, even our faith.*

If we have accepted Christ as Lord and Savior, we have already won the war. What war? The one that Satan is leading. He is trying to destroy our lives and our souls, but because of our faith, we are already victors.

However, there are battles that we must fight daily, and the outcome of those is dependent on our Christian walk. Tired of fighting a losing battle? Read on.

First of all, we must walk in God's Word. The Bible is *quick, and powerful, and sharper than any two-edged sword.* It is the weapon Jesus chose to fight with when He was tempted by Satan in the wilderness. It gives us joy, hope, peace, guidance, comfort, and much more. Without God's Word, we don't stand a chance of winning our daily battles. We must spend time in the Scriptures. We need to read the Bible and memorize verses that we can use to send the devil fleeing from us.

Second, we need to walk in God's will. If we follow our own will instead of God's, we're fighting the battle alone, and we're destined to fail. Yes, God is always with us, and He is our helper. However, if we're walking in our own will, we're acting in our own strength and not in the Lord's. It isn't that God left us. It's that we left Him. Often times, we do this without even realizing it. We see something we want, and we go for it without even taking the time to see if it is God's will for us to have it. We often forget that God sees the "Big Picture" of our lives and not just our current circumstances. He knows what is best for us, and He will lead us in the right direction. It's up to us to follow.

Third, we need to walk in God's world. Let's face it. We live in dark times. War and violence are everywhere. Sin has run rampant. Goodness is seen as weakness and often taken advantage of. It is tempting to turn our backs on this wicked world and just live our lives the best we can in isolation. But is that what God wants us to do? No! Until the return of Christ, it is our job to try to reach out to this lost and dying world. It is our responsibility to see people as God sees them: people in need of salvation. We must be witnesses, not out of duty, but out of love and compassion. By reaching out, not only can we win some of our battles, but we can help others to win theirs as well.

If you feel like you're fighting a losing battle or like you're simply spinning your wheels in life, the first thing to check is your Christian walk. Only by keeping ourselves in God's Word, in His will, and in His world can we walk in a winner's wonderland. It's not easy, but there is joy in the journey when we do!

MY TRIP TO OLD FAITHFUL

Yesterday, I visited Old Faithful. No, I'm not talking about the punctual geyser in Yellowstone National Park. I'm actually referring to my laundry basket. It seems to erupt just as faithfully. I don't get it. There are only two of us (well, two of us that wear clothing, although I'm beginning to suspect that the dogs play "dress up" every time Jason and I leave the house). How can the laundry basket always be full to the point of overflowing?

Unfortunately, the kitchen sink is the same way. No matter how many dishes I wash, there are always more to take their place. What? Do these things breed like rabbits?

As I tend to the "Old Faithfuls" in my life, I realize that our spiritual walk is very similar. Each time we think we've conquered a sin, it erupts in our lives again. Each time we think we've grown in Christ, we find ourselves acting like spiritual toddlers, throwing temper tantrums and whining to get our way. Just like my dishes and my laundry basket, no matter how many times

I "conquer" the problem, new ones seem to always be on the ready to act as replacements.

The truth is that unless my husband and I decide to stop wearing clothes (let's not go there), the laundry will never be finished. And unless we decide to stop eating (not likely), there will always be dishes to wash. Even so, unless we stop walking our spiritual walk (which shouldn't be an option), there will always be new giants to face.

Does it mean that we haven't made progress? Even though it may seem like it, no. What it really means is that we haven't quit. We're still running the race. We haven't given up on account of the obstacles. I know that sometimes our effort seems to be in vain, but one day, when we stand before the Lord and hear Him say, "Well done, thou good and faithful servant," we'll discover that it was worth it all. So, go out today and conquer some geysers in your life!

And God is able to make all grace abound toward you; that ye always having all sufficiency in all things, may abound to every good work - II Corinthians 9:8

WHISTLING A DIFFERENT TUNE

Go get your Bible. Really. I'll wait. Got it? Now, turn to Psalm 73 and read it. Did you see the pity party Asaph was having for himself. Unfortunately, it sounds like ones I've had myself (and more often than once). It goes something like this:

"God, why do the wicked get whatever they want? They constantly disobey You, yet they have more money, nicer homes, and nicer cars than I could ever dream of having. They seem to have perfect lives, and it's just not fair. I try to serve You every day, but I'm still struggling just to make ends meet."

Sound familiar? Come on, admit it. You've thrown one of these parties yourself, haven't you? If we're honest, I think we've all had these thoughts at least once in our lives. But what I really want to point out is the change that comes in verse 17. *Until I went into the sanctuary of God; then understood I their end.* At this point, Asaph's pity party has turned into a praise party.

Asaph finally turned his eyes away from himself, and he focused his attention on God. What a difference it made! He spends the rest of the chapter praising God for what He has done and what He will do. Asaph ends the chapter by saying, *But it is good for me to draw near to God.* Amen to that!

So, if you're in the midst of a glorious pity party, get your eyes off of yourself and your circumstances. Instead, look to God who is much greater than any situation you may be in. Call on His name. Give Him praise. Thank Him in advance for the blessings that He has yet to give you, and don't forget to give thanks for the many blessings you've already received. As Asaph said, it is good to draw near to God, and you can't do that and throw yourself a pity party at the same time.

It is true that life is not always fair, but it is also true that God is just. He will make all things right. After all, if we have Him, we truly have all that we need.

Whom have I in heaven but thee? and there is none upon earth that I desire beside thee. - Psalm 73:25

SOUNDS TOO GOOD TO BE TRUE?

We've all heard the saying, "If it sounds too good to be true, it probably is." I get a good dose of that daily. Being a freelance writer, I have to focus a lot of time on marketing and advertising, which means I see a lot of ads for other products. The hype online today is unbelievable!

Make $2,500 today. Guaranteed! No experience required!

Start your own business today and be a millionaire by the end of the month!

Grab this FREE report and find out how to have thousands of customers beating down your door!

Make $300-$500 every hour filling out simple forms! Even a child could do this!

Blah, blah, blah! Heard it. Seen it. Unfortunately, I've even tried some. The outcome? They didn't work. There's always some catch or some fine print. There's always some important tidbit of information that they conveniently leave out (but of course you can purchase that information for a small fee of $29.99). I get utterly disgusted seeing this junk every day! The bad part is that it gives a bad name and reputation to those of us who are truly marketing something honest. Some days it's just more than I can stand, and I allow myself to become discouraged and depressed.

It's then that I am reminded of God's promises. They sound too good to be true, but they are true! God doesn't lie. If He said He will do something, He will! Oh, what a joy to know that there's something real to rely on. What a relief to know that there's no fine print or missing information. God's Word spells out His promises loud and clear, and the best part is that He sticks to His Word. God keeps His promises. There's no hype involved!

Thy mercy, O LORD, is in the heavens; and thy faithfulness reacheth unto the clouds. - Psalm 36:5

RESTING WITH MY MASTER

I think my dog has ADHD. Mitch is an 90-lb. Shepherd mix, and I'm beginning to think he's mixed with the Energizer bunny. There is just no end to his energy. When he runs through the house, he breaks the sound barrier. He jumps. He dances. He even sings (I didn't say it was pretty). But of all the things Mitch loves to do, three favorites stand out.

First, he loves to eat. It doesn't matter what kind of food or treat it is, that boy can chow down! I think he should have been named Hoover because he vacuums up everything in sight.

Second, he loves to go for walks. We have to be very careful not to say the word unless we're ready to walk out the door with him because he goes CRAZY. He howls and growls until we put the leash on and take him out. He loves to walk, run, and even hike. He's very active and agile, so he really enjoys getting to go off and explore.

Third, he loves to stretch out between Jason's legs and sleep with his head in Jason's lap. Often, at the end of the day, we'll lie in bed and watch re-runs online. Mitch loves this time because he knows that during this time, he gets a lot of his daddy's attention. He rests in Jason's lap while Jason pets him. It doesn't take long for Mitch to fall asleep. It's really sweet (until the snoring begins).

The other night, we were just getting settled into bed when we noticed a large nose and a pair of eyes at the end of the bed. We acknowledged Mitch and told him he could come up. He jumped on the bed and with an enthusiasm I'd rarely seen walked right up to "his spot" and plopped down, closing his eyes in complete contentment.

The scene made me wonder if I'm that enthusiastic when I rest with my Master. Am I too busy to be content simply resting in His warm embrace? Do I come to Him with joy and excitement, eager to spend time with Him? Do I go to Him often enough that I have my own "spot"?

It's something worth pondering. The more I think about it, the more I realize that Mitch and I have a lot in common. I love to eat! I love to walk and hike (although I don't care much for running). And, I too, love to rest in the lap of my

Master. I only pray that I can do it with as much enthusiasm as Mitch does.

Come unto me, all ye that labour and are heavy laden, and I will give you rest. - Matthew 11:28

A WORD FITLY SPOKEN

A man hath joy by the answer of his mouth: and a word spoken in due season, how good is it! - Proverbs 15:23

Pleasant words are as an honeycomb, sweet to the soul, and health to the bones. - Proverbs 16:24

I think we all know at least one person who could use an encouraging word today. Right? So, when was the last time you sought to encourage someone? Did you visit that shut-in to brighten her day? Did you call that sick friend to wish him well? Did you get in touch with that family member in need to remind her that she is in your prayers? Did you send the card or e-mail? Convicting, isn't it? I know I'm guilty.

You see, life is hard and busy. We are so often preoccupied with just getting through each day that we forget that someone may be struggling more than we are. When we help that person by encouraging them, not only are they blessed, but we are too, and we find our own way is not as difficult as it seemed before. There is great joy in lifting someone up, so I encourage you today to contact someone, whether it be by phone, mail, e-mail, or even text message. Get in touch with at least one person today and let him know that you're thinking about him and praying for him. (Of course, if you say you're praying for him, make sure you are!)

Try to make this part of your daily routine. Each day, pray for the Lord to put someone who needs encouragement on your heart. Then, reach out to her and remind her that someone cares. Sometimes, being reminded that we're not alone makes all the difference in the world!

A word fitly spoken is like apples of gold in pictures of silver. - Proverbs 25:11

PROMISES AND POSSIBILITIES

We had a guest speaker at our church last night, and he brought a wonderful lesson on how all things are possible with God. He went through the Gospels and pointed out the number of times God had said in one way or another that all things were possible through Him and by Him. Check it out:

Matthew 19:26 - But Jesus beheld them, and said unto them, With men this is impossible; but with God all things are possible.

Mark 9:23 - Jesus said unto him, If thou canst believe, all things are possible to him that believeth.

Mark 10:27 - And Jesus looking upon them saith, With men it is impossible, but not with God: for with God all things are possible.

Mark 14:36a - And he said, Abba, Father, all things are possible unto thee.

Luke 18:27 - And he said, The things which are impossible with men are possible with God.

I don't believe God wastes words. I think He repeats Himself because we need that repetition. We need to be reminded that all things are possible. No matter how dark the valley we are facing, nothing is impossible with God. What a great promise!

I'M SO CONFUZZLED!

I've been researching the fitness industry for information to use on a new fitness program review website. All I can say is that there are as many fitness theories as there are stars in the sky. I'm serious! Low fat. Low carb. No meat. Only meat. Moderate exercise. Intense exercise. Workout daily. Workout two to three times each week. Not only that, but each one claims that their program is unquestionably the best, and some of them even contradict themselves if you read enough of the material. It's been frustrating, to say the least.

I'm so glad that when I sit down to read my Bible each day it doesn't contradict itself. I'm so thankful that the Word of God is true and that it is constant. It doesn't change from day to day depending on new theories or statistics. It's not watered down to be more appealing to the masses. From day to day, it stands. Am I saying that I completely understand everything in the Bible? Of course not! I don't think anyone does except for the Author. But when I open my Bible, I'm not bombarded by errors and inconsistencies. I'm not overwhelmed by contradictions. The Bible says what it means and it means what it says. Case closed!

When reading the various health and fitness manuals, I've learned to not put much stock in any of the information. After all, it may change on the next page. When reading my Bible, however, I'm confident taking in every word, for each one is important, and the message is unchanging!

Heaven and earth shall pass away; but my words shall not pass away.
- Luke 21:33

WHY MUST IT BE SO COMPLICATED?

Have you ever noticed how many books about prayer are out there? There are books on how to pray, when to pray, where to pray, and on and on. Now, as a writer, I love books, and I love to read. I'll admit that at this very moment, I have several prayer books on my bookshelf. There are many that I've read and really enjoyed. There are others that I've purchased but haven't yet had the opportunity to read. In my mind, books on any topic are great. I love books!

However, do you ever get the feeling that we sometimes over-complicate things? For example, in one book, the author comments that every successful Christian prays first thing in the morning. Another author comments that it's best to end your day with a conversation with the Lord. One book says that prayer should be friendly and conversational. Another advises it should be holy and reverent. Many books use the Lord's Prayer as a guide and then give an outline of what to say and when in your prayer to say it. It's no wonder so many of our prayer lives suffer!

God is not the author of confusion. Prayer is not supposed to be complicated. If you're concerned about when to pray, the Bible is clear on that. I Thessalonians 5:17 says, *Pray without ceasing.* So when is the best time to pray? Anytime. All the time. As far as how to approach prayer, I've found the most comfort when I just come to Him in my current state. In other words, sometimes I need my Heavenly Father to wrap me in His arms and give me advice or direction. Sometimes, I need my Heavenly Husband to whisper words of love to me and to accept those endearments in return. Sometimes, I just need my Friend to listen to the burdens that are weighing heavy on my heart. Then, there are times that I need Mighty God to remind me of how great He is and what He can accomplish. I approach my prayer time differently depending on my need or state of mind.

That concept may or may not work for you, and that's fine. My point is that we don't want to make prayer time so complex that it's more of a drudgery than a joy. We should enjoy our conversations with the Lord instead of making them a glorified wish list or a step-by-step outline. If you're unsure how to simplify your prayer life, ask the Lord for guidance, then

LISTEN for His response. Remember, it takes two to have a conversation.

SMALL WORD, BIG MEANING

I think every Christian (and probably several non-believers) can quote from memory Proverbs 3:5-6. *Trust in the Lord with all thine heart; and lean not unto thine own understanding. In all thy ways acknowledge him, and he shall direct thy paths.* We've read it. We've studied it. We've heard sermons and Sunday School lessons on it. Why? Because these are two very important verses. The passage is an excellent reminder for us to trust God even when we don't understand what He's doing.

Often, this passage is given as encouragement in a time of great trial or suffering. However, today, I'd like to look at it from a different angle. If you will look at verse six, you'll see a tiny little word that has a huge meaning. Look carefully. It's easy to miss. *In **all** thy ways acknowledge him.*

You see, this passage is not just for times of trouble. It's for **all** times. We should constantly be trusting the Lord and seeking His guidance. It's a natural response to stop and seek God's will in times of confusion or tribulation, but in this passage, God is reminding us to always acknowledge Him, to always seek His advice.

Even more to the point, we're not just talking about big things like whether or not we should move to a new location or take a certain job. God says that even in the usual, mundane activities of everyday life, we should seek His face, acknowledge His presence, and ask for His guidance. So, whether we spend our day cleaning bathrooms, raising children, working a job outside the home, etc., we should trust in God and acknowledge His presence in our lives

It's easy to pray in the morning and ask God for help and guidance, then to go off and do our own thing, heedless to the voice of God. I know I've done it more times than I can count. Unsure of how to get everything done, I seek God's help. I ask Him to give me strength and to guide me from one task to the next. However, as soon as I say "Amen," I jump up and go about my day, struggling to make it through and wondering why God isn't helping me. Could it be that it's because I'm not acknowledging Him?

So, as you go about your tasks today, no matter how tedious or mundane they may seem, remember to place them in God's hands. Trust in Him and acknowledge Him. It will make even the most difficult or boring task seem pleasant because you'll realize you're doing it for Him.

Shew me thy ways, O LORD; teach me thy paths. Lead me in thy truth and teach me: for thou art the God of my salvation; on thee do I wait all the day. - Psalm 25:4-5

DON'T HANG UP YOUR HARP

By the rivers of Babylon, there we sat down, yea, we wept, when we remembered Zion. We hanged our harps upon the willows in the midst thereof. For there they that carried us away captive required of us a song; and they that wasted us required of us mirth, saying, Sing us one of the songs of Zion. How shall we sing the Lord's song in a strange land? - Psalm 137:1-4

What a sad story! I'm sure we all know what it's like to be so discouraged that all we can do is sit and wish for the "good old days." While this is a natural response, it is not a good response. Self-pity will get us nowhere.

If we are saved by the blood of Jesus Christ, we are not of this world. Therefore, we are in a strange land. So, if we were to follow the example of Israel, we ought to just hang up our harps, forget about the Lord's song, and spend the rest of our days mourning our plight in life. Does that sound like what the Lord would want us to do? Of course not!

My pastor once made the comment, "Our circumstances in life will change, but our song shouldn't." AMEN!!! No matter how bad life gets,

God is still good and still worthy of our praise. So often, though, when we're faced with hard times, the only song we want to sing is "Nobody Knows the Trouble I've Seen." Wrong! God knows, and He cares.

I don't like hard times any more than the next guy, but they're part of life. I've faced my share of troubles and trials in my life, and I'm embarrassed to say that a good number of those times, I hung up my harp, buried my face in my hands, and gave myself a glorious pity party. You know the problem with pity parties? I'm the only guest! What fun is a party without guests and presents and, of course, cake (chocolate, if I have my way)?

The point is that God is good all the time. Even if we're going through hard times, and we don't understand the path that God has for us, we can still sing Him a song. He loves to hear our songs, especially when we're in a strange land. It blesses His heart to see our love and devotion to Him. So, stand up, be strong, and hold onto that harp. You're going to need it!

O give thanks unto the Lord; for he is good: for his mercy endureth for ever. – Psalm 136:1

OBJECTS OF EXTREME DEVOTION

The idols of the heathen are silver and gold, the work of men's hands. They have mouths, but they speak not; eyes have they, but they see not; They have ears, but they hear not; neither is there any breath in their mouths. They that make them are like unto them: so is every one that trusteth in them. - Psalm 135:15-18

Often we think of idol worship as a thing of the past or something that is only observed in far-away countries. However, if you look up the definition of "idol," you'll find it means "an object of extreme devotion." Anything come to mind? How about television, internet, cell phones, shopping, eating, etc.?

In today's world, it is so easy to get sidetracked from our priorities. There are so many things screaming for our attention that they drown out the voice of God calling us to come and worship Him. Instead, we spend our time checking e-mail and working on our "My Space" pages. When that's done, we plop down in front of the television because we feel the need to relax. As long as we're just sitting there, we might as well have something to eat, too. Notice the trend?

When do we pull ourselves away from the many "objects of extreme devotion" and take the time to truly spend some time with God (who should be THE object of extreme devotion)? I'll be the first to admit that I've had my devotion time in such a hurry and with such a half-hearted effort that I questioned myself later if I had actually done my devotions. What's the point in that? If that's all we're gaining from our time with the Lord, why do we go through the motions at all? Habit? Guilt? Obligation?

Now, before you throw out your television set or swing a baseball bat through your computer, let me say that there's nothing wrong with any of these things. Things, in and of themselves, are not the problem. The problem occurs when we allow things to take priority over God in our lives, when we allow things to become our idols. We must be careful! Let's keep our priorities straight and keep our worship and devotion where it belongs. After all, God alone is worthy of our praise!

Thou shalt have no other gods before me. - Exodus 20:3

LORD, A LITTLE HELP PLEASE!

We are all familiar with Paul's thorn in the flesh. Granted, we don't know specifically what it was. I know many believe it was a health issue of some kind, like blindness perhaps. We can't be certain, but we do know it often hindered him in his service to God. That makes me wonder.

Have you ever questioned why God would give us thorns in the flesh that prevent us from serving Him at our greatest capacity? Paul said it was so that he wouldn't be exalted above measure, but is that reason the same for all of us?

I know of godly people who can't make it to church because of physical ailments. I know of others who can't come to many events because they are needed to care for a loved one who is suffering from physical illness. I, myself, am constantly battling various physical conditions. During these times of suffering, I turn my face toward Heaven and cry, "Why, God? Couldn't I serve You better without this thorn? Don't You want the complete service that I could offer if I were healed?"

The answer I receive is the same as the one Paul received: *My grace is sufficient for thee: for my strength is made perfect in weakness. - 1 Corinthians 12:9a*

I don't understand God's ways, but I'm sure He knows what He is doing. So, for all of you who are suffering physically or taking care of those who are suffering physically, take heart. It's not easy, but God's grace will be sufficient. We don't need to understand; we only need to trust.

Therefore I take pleasure in infirmities, in reproaches, in necessities, in persecutions, in distresses for Christ's sake; for when I am weak, then am I strong. - II Corinthians 12:10

A REALLY BIG BOTTLE

I am a VERY tenderhearted person. I think sometimes that I'm too tenderhearted. I can't watch someone cry without joining them. If I see someone hurting, my heart aches for them. I can't even watch a touching movie (or commercial for that matter) without crying my eyes out. It just doesn't take much to make me cry.

For that reason, whenever I read verse 8 of Psalm 56, my mind begins to spin. It says, *Thou tellest my wanderings: put thou my tears into thy bottle: are they not in thy book?* I'm wondering if God keeps all of our tears. If so, does he keep them all in one bottle, or do we each have our own bottle? Even if I have my own personal tear bottle in Heaven, can you imagine how big it must be? I know that I've cried oceans of tears in my life, and I just can't imagine a bottle big enough to hold them all. It's an interesting thought, isn't it?

There is one thing I do know for sure. God sees each of my tears, and more than that, He understands each one. During those times when I just can't find the words to express how I feel, my tears can speak for me. What a blessing to know that God understands! What an even bigger blessing to know that one day, He will wipe all the tears from our eyes. We won't need them anymore. So, I wonder, what will happen to our tear bottles then?

WHAT DID I SAY?

Have you ever found yourself singing a song but not really paying attention to what you're singing? I've had times when I lifted my voice in joyous song, the words were rolling off my tongue, but the meaning was completely lost to me. It's not that I didn't understand what I was singing. It's just that I wasn't paying attention. Don't look at me that way. I know you've done the same thing. How many times have we stood in church and sung, "I Surrender All" without heeding the promise we were making?

In Psalm 47:7, the author says, *For God is the King of all the earth: sing ye praises with under-standing.* Did you catch that? Don't just sing it; mean it! That might limit our song choices a little. Won't it? For example, there's a song that I absolutely refuse to sing. It's a beautiful song entitled "Whatever It Takes." The song basically tells the Lord that I will be willing to do anything or give up anything for Him. Not just that, but that I'll do it gladly. I'd love to say that I know for a fact that I am in that position. However, when I think of Job, I ask myself if I'm REALLY willing to face that. I want to be, but I don't think I've arrived at that place yet. So, I don't sing the song because if I did, it would be a lie.

I often hear people comment on a particular song, about how beautiful the music is and how much they like it. Then, when I hear it, I discover that the lyrics are the complete opposite of the Scriptures. The doctrine is messed up or the message is just wrong! Is it a beautiful song because the music is pretty? Oh, we'd better be careful.

The Bible encourages us over and over again to sing praises unto the Lord. But if we don't mean it, we shouldn't sing it. So, to keep from making this mistake, we would do well to pay attention to what we are singing. Sing? Yes! But, sing with understanding.

Make a joyful noise unto God, all ye lands: sing forth the honour of his name: make his praise glorious. - Psalm 66:1-2

CHOCOLATE: THE FORBIDDEN FRUIT

For my devotions, I've been reading through the book *Becoming the Woman God Wants Me to Be* by Donna Partrow. I recommend it to all you ladies out there who look at the Proverbs 31 woman and say, "How in the world did she get it all done?" This book explores that question in great detail. It is a 90-day journey to becoming the virtuous woman spoken of in Proverbs 31. Each day's lesson contains Scripture memorization, Scripture reading, a short devotional, a daily affirmation, and some practical steps to take that day toward becoming "the new you." I've really enjoyed it. . . until this week.

This week, the author had the nerve to talk about our eating habits. Not a good topic for me! My idea of a balanced meal is a Reese's cup in each hand. I struggle constantly with maintaining healthy eating habits. Now, before I go any farther, I know many of you are saying, "Yeah, right. You're so skinny." Well, I'm not as skinny as I used to be. Plus, health is not always about the way we look. Often, it's about how we feel. That's where I suffer the most.

You see, I'm not one of those people who just can't stop eating. In fact, I don't usually eat that much. My problem is not how much I eat, but what I eat. There should be a Bible verse that reads, "Man cannot live by chocolate and caffeine alone." And the really bad part is that it's a vicious cycle with me. When I don't get the foods I need, I become depressed. When I'm depressed, I eat the foods I'm not supposed to have. Around and around we go!

So, you can imagine my response to this morning's devotion, in which Donna points out that the very first sin was caused by a woman being tempted by something that looked good to eat. OUCH! How many times have I fussed at Eve and wondered *Why did you have to eat that fruit?* Now, I see that if it had been me, I would have probably failed just as Eve did (especially if the forbidden fruit had been chocolate). From now on, every time I sit down with my chocolate cake, I'm going to feel guilty. Stupid book!

No, I'm just kidding. It's actually a very good book. I just don't like having my security blanket taken away from me. I don't like being told, "No! That's wrong!" I'm not saying that we should never eat sweets, but I know that I would certainly benefit from replacing some of my sweets with fruits and vegetables. No, they don't taste as good, but they are much better for me.

I need to constantly remind myself that my body is the temple of the Holy Ghost. I must take care of it. Feeding it unwholesome foods is just as detrimental to it as smoking or drinking. For me, this is the ultimate challenge, but it is a challenge I have to face. Who will face it with me?

What? know ye not that your body is the temple of the Holy Ghost which is in you, which ye have of God, and ye are not your own? - 1 Corinthians 6:19

KNOW YOUR AUDIENCE

Psalm 23 is a very familiar psalm. In fact, I think believers and non-believers alike have heard it so many times that they can quote it from memory. Memorization is great, but we must be careful to not allow the words to lose their meaning. When we quote a verse, are we just reciting the words or are we really thinking about what the verse is saying?

While doing my Bible reading this morning, I read through this familiar psalm. I was almost through when I realized I wasn't paying attention to what I was reading. My eyes saw. My lips spoke. My brain? Well, it was somewhere else. So, I went back and started reading again, and I saw something I had never noticed before. In the hundreds of times I've read, heard, and quoted it, I've never seen this. It's amazing what happens when you actually pay attention!

In verses 1-3, David is talking **about** the Lord. "The Lord is. . ." "He maketh. . ." "He restoreth. . ." But, look at what happens in verse 4. He completely changes his point of view or point of reference. Beginning in verse 4, David is actually talking **to** the Lord. "Thou art with me." "Thou preparest. . ." What happened between verses 3 and 4? Why the change?

Could it be that in the writing of this psalm, David remembered how precious the Lord is? Is it possible that he suddenly remembered that the Lord was there with him? Perhaps, David's change had to do with familiarity. After all, verse 4 talks about walking through the valley of the shadow of death. David had been there. Maybe, these verses meant so much to David because they reminded him that he was not alone. It could be as simple as the fact that he wrote it the way God told him to. I don't know, but I find it very interesting. There are many changes like this throughout the Psalms. Read a few, and you'll see what I'm talking about. In the first half of many of the chapters, David is questioning God. He spells out his complaints and troubles. He describes the trials he's facing and wonders why God won't help him. But then in the next verse, he's praising God and singing songs. Wouldn't you love to know what happened between those verses? Did David just resolve to be thankful? Or did God come down and thump him on the head, telling him to quit his griping?

(Don't laugh. God's done it to me a time or two.)

What's my point? First of all, when reading God's Word, pay attention. It is so easy to let our minds drift, but when we do, we miss out on something special. Second, look for God's work between the lines. Even if we can't figure out what the work is, it's a reminder to us that God is always in control, and He is always working in our best interest. If that's not worth paying attention for, I don't know what is.

Study to shew thyself approved unto God, a workman that needeth not to be ashamed, rightly dividing the word of truth. - II Timothy 2:15

REFLECTING THE LORD

As for me, I will behold thy face in righteousness: I shall be satisfied, when I awake, with thy likeness. - Psalm 17:15

In this passage, I don't think David is referring to a physical likeness. Instead, I think he is referring to the time when his words, thoughts, and actions reflect the Lord. He is stating that he won't be satisfied until he is a true picture of God Himself. What a challenge!

While some of my words, thoughts, and actions reflect the Lord, I have not arrived at the place where I can look at myself and see Him. I still have a lot of areas to work on before my character resembles that of Christ. And until then, I won't be satisfied. Until the world can see Jesus, and only Jesus, in me, I must keep striving to grow more like Him. How? Through prayer, Bible study, and walking with Him day by day. The task will not be easy, but the reward will truly be worth it!

But grow in grace, and in the knowledge of our Lord and Saviour Jesus Christ. To him be glory both now and for ever. Amen. - II Peter 3:18

GOD'S WAYS ARE NOT MY WAYS

This morning I went outside for my devotions. I was reading and meditating when out of the corner of my eye, I saw this white blur. I turned to see my dog, Mitch, running as fast as he could run with his long white rope dangling from his mouth. (Yes, he has his own rope.) He made circles around the yard, running and growling. I can't describe the sight to you, but it was so funny that I laughed uncontrollably. The more he ran around, the harder I laughed. The more I laughed, the more he wanted to run. I guess he liked the approval.

I looked at Tippy, my older dog, who was just staring at Mitch like he'd lost his mind. "He's a mess. Isn't he?" I said to her. (Yes, I talk to my dogs. Get over it.) But then the thought hit me of how much we enjoy having Mitch as part of our family. He's a real joy. That thought in itself isn't strange, but the thought that followed was. We never would have gotten Mitch if Tessa, our first dog, hadn't passed away.

I believe Tessa's passing was God's way of directing us to another one of His creatures that needed love and care. If you had seen Mitch when he was at the pound, it would have broken your heart. I've seen a lot of "puppy dog eyes," but he was truly pitiful. I've never seen anyone or anything look as lost and abandoned as he did. Today, he doesn't even look like the same dog. He is happy and energetic, lovable and rotten.

He will never take Tessa's place, and I don't think God intended for him to. But I do believe God worked this out, even though it's hard to understand and even sometimes hard to accept. I love Mitch. In just the few months we've had him, he has wiggled his way into my heart, and life with him is VERY interesting. I would love to have my Tessa back, but I see now that the Lord was working things for the good. It is true that God's ways are not our ways. The sooner we accept that, the better off life will be.

For my thoughts are not your thoughts, neither are your ways my ways, saith the LORD. - Isaiah 55:8

HAS ANYONE SEEN MY BROOM?

Is it just me or are the weekends busier than the weekdays? Don't get me wrong. I had a very pleasant weekend: hiking with the hubby, my niece's birthday party, wonderful church services. It just seems like no matter how busy I stay during the week, there's still so much to do on the weekend. For example, right now my house is in DESPERATE need of a good cleaning. I could have done it this weekend. I could have tried to squeeze it in, but frankly, I didn't want to. Instead, on Friday afternoon, Jason and I dropped everything and went on a hike at Table Rock. On Saturday, we did a few errands in the morning, then went to my niece's birthday party. When we left there, we went shopping for new hiking boots. (If you haven't noticed, we do a lot of hiking.) Sunday, we had church in the morning and evening, and in the afternoon, we sat in the bed and watched reruns online.

You're probably wondering why I'm telling you all of this. Well, if anyone is familiar with the "Martha syndrome," I certainly am. Work, work, work. No joy. No life. No fun! If you have no idea what I'm talking about, look up Luke 10:38-42.

Martha was careful and troubled. Ever been there? Me, too. Why? Because she totally lost sight of what was important.

Please understand, I'm not saying that watching television is more important than cleaning your house. I'm saying that if we're always working and we never have any fun, frankly we become no fun to be around. A few weeks ago, I saw a "me" that I didn't like. She had no joy. She complained all the time. She was irritated and irritable. She was no fun to be around at all. I didn't even like being around her, but I found it difficult to get away from her. I came to the conclusion that I had been trying too hard to make everything perfect (I'm bad about that), and in the meantime, I was driving myself (and others) crazy. Why? EVERYTHING CAN'T BE PERFECT! Whew! I said it. But better yet, I'm finally believing it.

The house is a mess today, and it will probably still be a mess tomorrow, but you know what? Who cares? I spent an hour in precious communion with my Lord today. I played with my two sweet puppies in the backyard. I sent an anniversary card to my parents and a card of encouragement to a dear friend. I did a good deal of my writing outside, enjoying the beautiful weather. Tonight, Jason and I plan to continue our search for hiking boots. Aren't these things much more important than having a spotless house?

Priorities—we all have them. Now we just need to get them in the right order. Please don't spend your entire day working. We all have to work. I understand that. I actually got a good bit of writing done today, but because I took time for the other things that were important, I'm in a much better mood and I feel that I've accomplished so much more! Do something for yourself today. You are no good to anyone if you're exhausted and irritated. Find what is needful in your life, and hold on to it with an unyielding grip.

JUST BE QUIET

In Job 39, after Job's pity party, the Lord is questioning him, proving that He alone is all-powerful, and He alone is in control. The Lord ends His questioning with this: *Shall he that contendeth with the Almighty instruct him? he that reproveth God, let him answer it.*

The part I like is Job's answer. *Behold, I am vile; what shall I answer thee? I will lay mine hand upon my mouth.* In other words, "I'll shut up now!"

I think we all need that reminder every now and then. Don't we? Often times, we see a situation and think we know the best way to solve it. So when God leads us in another direction, we argue with Him, stating our points and reasons. At times like that, God has to pull us down from our self-appointed pedestals and say, "Who do you think you are? Do you control the world, or do I?" Umm . . . good point! Who are we to instruct God in the way things should be done?

And the principle of keeping our mouths shut doesn't stop there. I know we've all had times when we said things that we should have kept to ourselves. You know the routine: the thought pops into your head, you know you shouldn't say it, but your desire to have the last word overcomes all else, and then you blurt it out and are immediately regretful. But it's too late. The harm has already been done. Many times, we would be so much better off if we would learn to keep our mouths shut. If we feel we must have the last word, let's make it a word of encouragement or an apology. If that's not possible, it's better to just walk away. Cool off! Let our anger dissipate. But whatever we do, let's keep a rein on our tongue. It can truly be a dangerous weapon.

To everything there is a season, and a time to every purpose under the heaven. . . a time to keep silence, and a time to speak. - Ecclesiastes 3:1,7b

IT'S OUR CHOICE

This morning I was getting breakfast for my dogs. Mitch wakes up each morning with a growling tummy, so he's very adamant about getting his breakfast. Tippy loves to eat as well, but she has a hard time getting down off the bed by herself. I've discovered that it's easier to fix their breakfast with only one dog dancing around me instead of two, so I leave Tippy on the bed until I have their bowls ready. I set Mitch's bowl on the floor, and while he's eating, I'll get Tippy and then set her bowl on the floor. This usually works well.

This morning, I brought Tippy out, but she immediately left her eating spot and came to me in the kitchen where I was fixing my breakfast. *That's odd*, I thought. Tippy NEVER leaves food behind.

"Go eat your food," I prodded her. No luck. "If you don't hurry, Mitch will eat it." Still she stood there begging for my breakfast. "No," I chided, "this is my breakfast. You go eat your own food." She wouldn't budge.

Finally, I walked her over to her bowl. . . only her bowl wasn't there. It was still sitting on the counter where I had set it to fix their breakfast. I laughed at myself, set the food on the floor, and she immediately started chowing down. (Don't laugh at me. I know you've done something similar. Admit it!)

Unlike Tippy, many times we go hungry and it's no one's fault but our own. I'm not speaking of being physically hungry. I'm talking about spiritual malnutrition. God has prepared a feast for us to sit down to every day. The Word of God. The Bread of Life. It's there for the taking. Whether we eat or not is up to us. God has prepared the meal and placed it in front of us. From there, it's up to us. Eat or don't eat. It's our choice.

This is my comfort in my affliction: for thy word hath quickened me. - Psalm 119:50

THE POTTER KNOWS THE CLAY

Do you ever find yourself praying, "God, what are You doing?" Do you ever wonder why life has to be so difficult? Do you ever feel so weary in well doing that you just don't feel you can go on? I know those feelings well, for I've walked through the valley. You know the feeling—everything is going well, you're serving the Lord to the best of your ability, you feel you're making progress, and then BAM! Suddenly, you find yourself back where you started and staring at the same obstacles you've faced so many times before.

Sometimes life if just SO confusing! In my case, I struggle with making things fit. My schedule is busy and complicated. My health is fair, but it could use some help. I find myself running out of energy long before I run out of time. And joy in the journey? It exists, but sometimes I have a hard time remembering what it's like. The problem is that I've been so busy living that I've forgotten to just enjoy life.

As Jason held me in his arms last night, I sobbed and exclaimed, "I don't enjoy anything anymore. I feel like everything I do is just another task to check off my to-do list." How sad, yet how true. I'm approaching life completely the wrong way. The real problem is that I've become so used to my "routine," it's going to take a lot of work to get me out of it.

As I lay in bed this morning, praying and asking God to show me the answers, He brought a song to my mind. It speaks of how the Potter knows the clay and exactly how much heat it can take before it cracks. It's a beautiful song, and quite an encouragement! What I am going through is not abnormal or unnatural. It's just some time in the fire, as God is molding me and making me into what He wants me to be. It's going to take time, and my job is to allow myself to be molded. Will it be easy? No, but I can rest in the promise that I won't have to face the fire alone.

He giveth power to the faint; and to them that have no might he increaseth strength. Even the youths shall faint and be weary, and the young men shall utterly fall: But they that wait upon the Lord shall renew their strength; they shall mount up with wings as eagles; they shall run, and not be weary; and they shall walk, and not faint.
- Isaiah 40:29-31

IT'S NOT ABOUT ME

In my devotional reading this morning, I was reminded of a "revelation" I experienced several months back. I was preparing for my Sunday School lesson on the topic of seeing ourselves as God sees us. The lesson basically contrasted an arrogant, self-satisfied attitude with an attitude of worthlessness and low self esteem. One of the follow-up questions was "What sin is the source of an arrogant, self-satisfied attitude?" Duh! Pride. The next question was "What sin is the source of an attitude of worthlessness and low self-esteem?" Hmm. That's a tough one. The answer? Pride.

It's easy to see pride in that person who thinks he is the center of the universe. But the person who constantly questions his self-worth is also exhibiting pride. How? Look at his focus. He is focused on one thing: self. I am not worthy. I am so dumb. I am so worthless. When we are focused on self, whether inflating or deflating, we are full of pride.

That lesson hit me hard because I always thought I was safe from pride because I tend toward lower self-esteem. It rocked my boat to find out that I was being just as proud as the person who boasts of his many accomplishments.

So, what does it mean to see ourselves through God's eyes? First of all, we are His creation, which means we are under His authority. In other words, it's His way, not our way. Secondly, anything we accomplish, we do so through His power and not our own. If we keep these things in mind, that should help with the arrogant spirit. As for the other, none of us is worthy of God's goodness if we come to Him in and of ourselves. Thankfully, we don't have to. When we look at ourselves, we see our sins and failures. We see creatures unworthy of mercy and grace. However, when God looks at us, He sees His children washed clean in the blood of the Lamb. In His eyes, we are worthy to come before Him.

You see, it's how He sees us and not how we see ourselves that is important. The book of Psalms does an excellent job in reminding us how precious we are to God and yet how much we need Him. So, when pride causes you to take a warped view of yourself, go to the book of Psalms and be reminded of how God views you. Trust me. It will be worth your time.

I will praise thee; for I am fearfully and wonderfully made; marvellous are thy works; and that my soul knoweth right well. - Psalm 139:14

A CHOCOLATE-CAKE KIND OF DAY

Have you ever had one of those days? You know, the kind where you just want to eat a large piece of chocolate cake and go back to bed. Today—or more specifically this morning—was one of those days. I got up early to make sure I wasn't late for my doctor's appointment. I left the house 30 minutes before my 10:00 appointment even though it only takes 15 minutes to get there. It was a good thing I left early.

Before I go any further, allow me to point out that I am horrible with directions. I get lost in the mall. (I wish I were making that up.) I know one way to get to the doctor's office. One way! That's it. Unfortunately, one of the roads that I needed to reach my destination was closed. Instant panic! I got out my GPS. It redirected me to where I basically turned myself in a circle and ended up back at the same "Road Closed" sign. (What good are those things anyway!) I grabbed my cell phone and called Jason. As the phone was ringing, I looked down at the clock on the dash. It read "9:45."

My loving husband pulled up a map on his computer at work and patiently navigated me around the closed road. (It didn't help that some of the roads I came to were not on his map. Who's responsible for that anyway? I'd like to talk with them.) I pulled into the parking lot at 9:58. Jason's final words to me were "Breathe, Dana, breathe."

I left the doctor's office at 11:00 (record time) and immediately called Jason. "I don't know how to get home," I mumbled into the phone. He laughed then guided me back to familiar territory. Once there, I decided to pick us up some lunch since he was starving and I was just in the mood to eat.

The trip to the store was amazingly quick, but on my way to drop off Jason's lunch at his work, I came across . . . you guessed it—"Road Closed." You have got to be kidding me!!!! I called Jason back, reminded him how thankful I was to work from home, and promised that after dropping off his lunch I was going home for good. The day has greatly improved since then.

In the book of Psalms, David says, *This is the day which the Lord hath made; we will rejoice and be glad in it.* It's hard to say that on days like today. However, as I study that Psalm, I can't help but notice that it doesn't say, "If things go our way, we will rejoice and be glad in it."

In other words, as Christians, every day should be a good day. Why? Because we've been redeemed! And in eternity, the street of gold will never be closed, so what does a little road construction matter down here?

Sing unto the LORD; for he hath done excellent things: this is known in all the earth. - Isaiah 12:2

DO YOU NEED SOME HELP LORD?

Last night at church, the pastor preached a message from Genesis 16. It's the story where Sarai grows tired of waiting on God to fulfill His promise, so she decides to take matters into her own hands. So, Abram has a child with Sarai's servant, Hagar. We are still reaping the consequences of this foolish act today.

Whenever I hear this story, I get so aggravated with Abram and Sarai. *Why couldn't you just wait on God?* I wonder. *Why did you think you knew better than He did? Didn't you trust Him to keep His promise?* But about half-way through my rant, I realize that I do the same thing day after day. I ask God for something. He promises to supply my needs. But if He doesn't answer within my time frame, I take matters into my own hands.

By taking control of the situation, not only do I miss out on a blessing from God, but I also make a mess of things. But that isn't even the worst part. While cleaning up my messes and licking my wounds, I have to ask myself, *Who else did this affect?* As I stated earlier, Abram's and Sarai's mistake is still causing massive trouble today. What kind of trouble are my mistakes causing?

Just this week, I have been fighting this battle again. I've begged the Lord to help me with a certain situation, but it seems that He hasn't heard me. My "natural man" wants to take control and say, *Fine! You won't help me; I'll help myself!* But the "spiritual man" is asking, *Lord, what are you trying to teach me during this time of waiting?* I can't listen to both. I must make a choice. I believe last night's sermon was for me. I believe God was reminding me to be careful, for when I try to take matters into my own hands, I may be hurting more than just myself. And that's not a risk I'm willing to take.

Trust in the Lord with all thine heart; and lean not unto thine own understanding. In all thy ways acknowledge him, and he shall direct thy paths. - Proverbs 3:5-6

HOPPING MAD

Have you ever been really irritated by someone or something? I'm talking irritated to the point where you can practically see smoke coming from your nostrils. I think I was there this morning.

Yesterday, I contacted a book club that I belong to and requested that they please cancel my account. I joined several months ago with the agreement that I would purchase at least four books from them in the next two years. To date, I have purchased eight. (This is not including the stuff that they sent me arbitrarily that I had to pay to return.)

This morning I received an e-mail from them stating that they were sorry but I could not cancel my membership at this time since I had not fulfilled my requirement. My first thought was *Can't you people count?* I was frustrated, but I sent a reply saying that if they would look on my account page on their own website, they would see that I had purchased far more than required.

They replied that not all of those books counted toward my requirement. What? Where was that fine print? When you order a book from their website, nowhere on there does it say whether or not that book will count toward your requirement. How is a person supposed to know what counts and what doesn't? In my mind, this is a very underhanded way of doing business.

The thing that really bothers me is that this is supposed to be a Christian company. I have had one problem after another since joining this club, which is why I wanted to cancel my membership. I'm about as non-confrontational as they come, but this drove me to the edge! I am tired of being taken advantage of.

The situation is still not resolved. I'm waiting to hear back from them . . . again. If nothing else, this situation has taught me to watch my steps carefully while naming the name of Christ. I am a reflection of Him and His love, and God forbid I should ever deal with people in such a misleading and deceiving manner.

If you claim to be a Christian, you'd better live it! People are watching!

Lie not one to another, seeing that ye have put off the old man with his deeds; and have put on the new man, which is renewed in knowledge after the image of him that created him. - Colossians 3:9-10

BE STILL

Psalm 46:10 says, *Be still, and know that I am God.* Of all the commandments given throughout the Bible, I think this is the hardest one for me to obey. I find it extremely difficult to be still. I feel the need to stay busy. After all, there is always something that has to be done. And when I can finally get my body to be still, my mind is running in circles. *Where should I send this article? How are we going to get all the youth to the Youth Retreat? What was it that I thought of earlier that I need to pick up from the grocery store? Boy, I blew it today!* And the list goes on and on. I feel like a hamster on an exercise wheel!

Why is it so important for us to be still anyway? Doesn't God want us to be productive? Yes, He does, but not to the extent that we lose our focus. God wants us to take some time to rest and to dwell on the fact that He is God. In other words: He is our Creator. He is our Helper. He is our Salvation. He is our King. He is our Friend. He is our Comforter. He is our Hope. He is our Counselor. To sum it all up, He is ALL we need.

If I'll just be still long enough to let that sink in, my life will be forever changed. *Be still, and know that I am God* It's not just a command. It's a necessity of life!

STILL, BE STILL

God works in mysterious ways. In fact, sometimes it's downright spooky! Earlier this week, I wrote the devotion entitled "Be Still." On Wednesday night, a friend gave me a card which I put in my purse and forgot about until this morning. I read it a few minutes ago. It talked about being still in the midst of hectic times. Yesterday morning in church, a ladies' trio sang the song "Stand Still." That was followed up by a guest speaker whose message was on. . .you guessed it. . .being still.

Do you ever get the feeling that God is beating you in the head with something? I often tell the Lord that I don't get subtle hints and that He must be very plain with me. Many times, I think God speaks to me in His still, small voice, but I'm too busy to hear. It's times like this that the same message seems to "pop up" everywhere I turn. I consider it God's way of getting my attention. And it works!

What's the moral of this story? Let us all pray that we never get too busy to hear the sweet voice of God. Let us pray that we are so in tune with Him that we know, without a doubt, His will for each of our lives. Let us take some time today to just be still and to bask in His presence, for He is worthy of our time and attention.

Be still, and know that I am God - Psalm 46:10

ROUND AND ROUND WE GO

In my devotions this morning, I was reminded of the importance of focusing on one thing at a time and doing each task to the best of my ability. In writing, it is so easy to lose focus. Should I work on my magazine article or my book? Do I need to set up my website or write my next e-book? What about reading? When should I do that? Some days, I find myself chasing my tail just trying to figure out what to work on next.

But focus is not only important in writing. It is imperative that we have focus in all areas of our lives. If our attention is split among several different things, are we able to devote our best to each of those? God wants us to do all things well and for His glory. We can't do that if we don't keep our focus.

I really need that reminder this morning. It's bound to be a busy day and the start of a busy weekend. Through my morning devotions, God reminded me that He will be with me every step of the way. All I need to do is focus on the next step.

Whatsoever thy hand findeth to do, do it with thy might. -
Ecclesiastes 9:10a

VENGEANCE IS MINE

I've been reading through the story of Esther. Today, I got to my favorite part—the part where Haman thinks he is about to receive a reward from the king only to be told that the reward is going to his hated enemy, Mordecai. I love it! Every time I read through the passage, I can see in my mind's eye Haman's expression as it changes from one of a cocky smirk to a look of total disbelief.

And as if vengeance wasn't well served at that point, the story goes on to tell how he was hanged on the very gallows that he had built for Mordecai. Justice is complete, and I couldn't have done it better myself!

This story always reminds me of Romans 12:19 which says, *Vengeance is mine; I will repay, saith the Lord.* So many times in life, we try to take justice into our own hands. When someone wrongs us, our fleshly nature feels the need to repay that wrong. Not only is this response bad because it often leads us to committing sin, but it is also wrong in that we are trying to take the place of God. Who are we to judge and determine punishment? We are not worthy of such a role.

To me, the story of Haman is always a reminder that God will handle the injustices in my life, and He will handle them far better than I ever could.

Arise, O God, judge the earth: for thou shalt inherit all nations. - Psalm 82:8

CHECK THE INGREDIENTS

Once a month, Jason and I will go to the bargain grocery store and check out what they've gotten in recently that we can use. For the most part, it's a "scratch and dent" kind of place, but you'd be amazed at the discount you can get on some of this stuff just because the cans are ugly.

Anyway, when we go, he tries to stock up on coffee because they carry brands that we usually can't afford at VERY good prices. His recent discovery was a lovely hazelnut blend. I love hazelnuts, and usually the smell of anything with hazelnut in it makes my mouth water. That was not the reaction I had yesterday morning when I first smelled the coffee.

"What's that smell?" I asked wrinkling my nose and trying to calm the tickle in the back of my throat. My first thought was that Jason had spilled some of the cinnamon deodorizer that he uses for work. (I'm allergic to cinnamon.) It didn't take me long to realize it was the coffee. I turned the coffee pot off and grabbed the new can of coffee, searching the label for the ingredients. Coffee, Natural and artificial flavors. Hmm, well, I can tell you what one of those flavors is.

I called Jason. "How was your coffee?"

"Great. It's really good. In fact, you might even like it." (No, he wasn't kidding. He didn't realize it had cinnamon in it.)

"No," I replied. "I don't think I'll care for it. In fact, I already don't like it." By this time, my throat was closing up, my eyes were watering, and I could feel a headache coming on. Even my own home is not cinnamon-proof this time of year. What's a girl to do?

As much as I hate it, Jason will have to give away a perfectly good can of coffee. (Anyone like hazelnut coffee with a touch of cinnamon?) This reminds me that in food, all does not necessarily work together for good.

In life, however, we are assured that God is in control. He sees the big picture. He knows the entire plan. He has His eyes on the beginning and the end. He will see that all things work together for good.

Things may not seem good now, but the rest of the story has not yet been told. God is in control of all the ingredients, and He will blend them together in a way that only He can to bring about a result that only He can imagine. Whatever you're going through today, be patient and trust that God will be true to His Word. Trust in His ingredients.

And we know that all things work together for good to them that love God, to them who are the called according to his purpose. - Romans 8:28

HIDDEN IN PLAIN VIEW

Hebrews 12:1-2 says, *Wherefore seeing we also are compassed about with so great a cloud of witnesses, let us lay aside every weight, and the sin which doth so easily beset us, and let us run with patience the race that is set before us, Looking unto Jesus the author and finisher of our faith; who for the joy that was set before him endured the cross, despising the shame, and is set down at the right hand of the throne of God.*

I have heard and read that passage so many times that I can quote it in my sleep. Yet it wasn't until recently that a part of it jumped out at me. Referring to Jesus, the Bible says, *who for the joy that was set before HIM* (emphasis mine). I had always read the words, but in my mind I was thinking of the joy that was set before us as Christians. What joy is set before Christ? After all, He left a place of perfect peace and joy to come and die on a cruel cross for our sins. Now, He is in Heaven again, but if that's the joy this verse is speaking of, why would He have left Heaven in the first place?

I believe that the joy spoken of here is the joy of knowing that He purchased our salvation and that, if we've accepted that gift, we will spend all eternity with Him. We are the joy that was set before Him. He is looking forward to spending eternity with us just as we are looking forward to spending it with Him. I don't know about you, but that new revelation has made this passage even more precious to me. Jesus is waiting for me with open arms and a huge smile on His face. The eternal celebration is imminent. Will you be there?

LIVING LIKE A MARSH-WIGGLE

I've been reading "The Silver Chair" by C.S. Lewis. One of the main characters in this particular book is a creature named Puddleglum, the Marsh-wiggle. He has kept me laughing through the entire book with his attitude. You see, he comments that all the other Marsh-wiggles tell him to get his head out of the clouds and to stop having such a positive attitude all the time, when, in fact, his attitude is anything but positive. He's constantly making comments like "No doubt, this is the last time we'll see each other." And, "We're likely to be eaten, I'll reckon." And, "What's food for Marsh-wiggles may be poison to humans, I should think." Each of these comments is made with such a dry tone and an obviously negative attitude. Without a doubt, this character honestly believes that bad things always happen and they will continue to happen. So every time Puddleglum makes some comment about looking on the bright side, I can't help but laugh because he thinks he's being positive.

But then I started thinking. Am I a Puddleglum? I admit I've had more than my share of negative moments when I was sure all hope was lost. And I further admit that I've counseled many a friend to just put the circumstances in God's hands, and He will handle the rest. It sounds to me that I, just like Puddleglum, am not practicing what I "preach." How can I be negative all the time, and then turn around and tell others to be positive?

I'm sure when C.S. Lewis wrote the Narnia series, he had no idea how much it was going to impact the world. There are so many lessons to be learned from these stories, and if you haven't read them, I encourage you to. While reading, look for the symbolism tied into each story. I'm sure it will bless you, and maybe even convict you as it has me.

A merry heart doeth good like a medicine. - Proverbs 17:22

HAVE YOU HAD YOUR CHOCOLATE "SON"DAY?

Building the perfect ice cream sundae is a creative process. Personally, I like to begin with a hot, fudgy brownie. On that, I place two scoops of chocolate ice cream, topped with nuts, chocolate sprinkles, chocolate cool whip, and if I'm feeling guilty, a shiny red cherry (for the nutritional value, of course).

Did you notice a trend? What can I say? I'm a chocolate lover, and if I'm going to make a sundae, I'm going to make it right. After all, sundaes are not served daily at my house. No, they are reserved for special occasions. They are intended for times of celebration.

At this point, may I suggest that every day should be a cause for celebration? The very fact that we woke up this morning is reason to celebrate. Life is a precious gift, yet we are often too busy or too preoccupied to notice it. Yes, we perform our daily tasks, but is that really living?

Don't get me wrong. I understand that we all have to work or to do things we really don't want to do, but how is our attitude during these times? Are we resentful that we have to work, or are we thankful that we have the health to perform a job? Attitude makes a big difference.

Picture in your mind a celebration. How many smiling faces do you see? How many people look like they're having fun? It's hard to be somber and gloomy in the middle of a party. Isn't it? Unless, of course, it's a pity party.

Now, picture your own life. See yourself doing the things that you do day after day. Are you smiling? Do you look like you're having fun? Are you enjoying life or simply enduring it?

In Psalm 118:24, David says, *This is the day which the Lord hath made; we will rejoice and be glad in it.* Notice, David didn't give any stipulations. He didn't say, "If it's a good day, we can rejoice." He didn't say, "If things go my way, I'll be glad in it." He simply said, "God made the day, so I'm going to rejoice in it." Case closed.

David understood the importance of celebrating life. Does that mean David didn't have any problems? Absolutely not! David's life had more twists and turns than a constipated snake. Nevertheless, David knew how to rejoice in the Lord during the good times and the bad times.

Some of you may be saying, "But you have no idea how difficult my life is." You're right. I don't know, but God does, and He will help you through those hard times. He promised that He would never leave us and that He would always meet our needs, whatever they may be. Is that not a good reason to celebrate?

Now, for those of you who already have the ice cream scoop in hand, let me say that I am not advocating indulging ourselves in ice cream sundaes each day. Instead, let's partake of "Son"days. Let's celebrate living by spending time with the One who gave us this gift of life. Praise! Thanksgiving! Worship! What a wondrous treat!

Christians, we should be the happiest people on earth. If we can't find a reason to celebrate, why would the lost want what we have? We have Jesus; therefore, we have joy. Let's not miss another opportunity to celebrate. Life may not

always be good, but it is always special. Have you
had your chocolate "Son"day today?

DR. JEKYLL AND MRS. HYDE

I received an e-mail this morning from a dear friend. The e-mail was entitled "Women of Influence." She wrote that she wanted me to read it because I was such a woman of influence, even if I didn't feel like it. My first thought was *Oh, if she only knew.* This made me question why that thought popped into my head, and it didn't take me long to find the answer.

I am the type of person who has no desire to be the center of attention or in the middle of a confrontation. For this reason, when I'm at church or out in the public, I do my very best to put on a "happy face," no matter what may be amiss in my life. This, in itself, is not a problem. The problem lies in the times when I'm at home, and, after holding in my feelings all day, I feel the need to do some serious venting. I complain about being wronged. I whine about getting my feelings hurt. I'm moody about something that didn't go my way. Woman of influence? Maybe. But the right kind? Not always. I'm sure if some of my dearest friends at church saw me in my own home sometimes, they would not recognize me as the same person. It's almost like I'm bipolar, swinging from one end of the mood spectrum to the other. From Tigger to Eeyore.

My prayer is that the Lord will help me to live up to the labels others have placed on me. I pray that what they see at church will be what I live each day. I implore Him to give me the strength to keep that "happy face" all the time and not just for the sake of appearances.

Create in me a clean heart, O God; and renew a right spirit within me. - Psalm 51:10

RIDING THE WORRY TRAIN

Wherefore seeing we also are compassed about with so great a cloud of witnesses, let us lay aside every weight, and the sin which doth so easily beset us, and let us run with patience the race that is set before us, looking unto Jesus the author and finisher of our faith; who for the joy that was set before him, endured the cross, despising the shame, and is set down at the right hand of the throne of God. - Hebrews 12:1-2

There's a lot of good stuff in those couple of verses, but I want to pull out one little phrase from verse one: *the sin which doth so easily beset us.*

Each of us has one particular sin that we battle over and over again. We work on that area of our life. We strive to make it better. We think we've almost arrived, and then, before we see what's happening, we find ourselves back at square one. I'm sure you know exactly what I'm talking about. For many, this sin is worry.

Most people refuse to acknowledge that worry is a sin. They fool themselves into believing that it is just an annoying habit and nothing more. But that's not what the Bible says. In fact, Romans 14:23 says, *And he that doubteth is damned if he eat, because he eateth not of faith: for whatsoever is not of faith is sin.* So, what is faith? The opposite of worry. This verse tells us quite plainly that if we doubt (or worry), it is a sin. If that's not proof enough, I could take you to many verses where God commands us to "fret not." What does "fret" mean? Worry!

The first problem with worry is that it takes our eyes off Christ and focuses them instead on our troubles. Big mistake! When we look at our problems, they seem so huge and unsolvable, but when we keep our eyes on Christ, we see how big and mighty He is. This doesn't make our problems go away, but it makes them a lot easier for us to handle.

The second big problem with worry is that it never travels alone. When we hop aboard the "worry train," we find ourselves facing doubt, discouragement, regret, and ingratitude.

In the first stage of worry, we begin to doubt ourselves, others, and even God. In our fretful state, we cling to the attitude that everyone is out to get us and that nobody cares about our problems.

That leads us to discouragement. We become so overwhelmed by our troubles that we sink into the deep abyss of depression. In that pit, we begin to re-examine our lives, pointing out all the things we could have or should have done differently. We find ourselves regretting past mistakes and decisions. Then we start to dwell on those, which only adds to our discouragement.

At that point, we are so consumed that we become ungrateful and even forgetful. We forget the many instances in the Bible where God provided for His children. We forget the many times He provided for us in the past. We become discontent with what we have and ungrateful for all the blessings we've been given. And in that ingratitude, we began to worry if God even cares about us at all.

Did you see what just happened? At the end of the "worry train," the process began all over again, and it will keep repeating until we deal with the problem.

Elijah the prophet is an excellent example of how the "worry train" works. In I Kings 18, Elijah takes on all of the prophets of Baal. At Elijah's request, God sends down fire to consume Elijah's sacrifice while the prophets of Baal can't even bring down a spark.

This display turned many hearts to the true God. You would think Elijah would have been elated. But in the very next chapter, when he discovers that Queen Jezebel wants him dead, he flees into the wilderness. There he pleads with the Lord to take his life, complaining that he is the only one left who wants to serve God. What happened?

First, Elijah became worried. He was afraid of what Jezebel might do to him. That worry led him to doubt God's ability to protect him, so he fled. At that point, he was all alone (except for God, of course), but that was by his own choice. He had nothing to do but to dwell on his circumstances. This led him deep into discouragement.

If you read his arguments with the Lord, you'll see his regret enter the picture. He basically tells the Lord that all his work was in vain because now he's the only one left. Do you detect a hint of ingratitude? Where is the thankfulness for the miracle God had just performed? Where was the gratitude for God's provision of food even when Elijah was running away from his responsibilities? When we're consumed with worry, we forget what God can do and what He's already done.

Now that we understand the "worry train," let's discuss how we can get off it. First, we must keep our hearts thankful. We must never forget what God can do or what He has already done. The best way to do this is to meditate on His Word day and night. Keep it in our hearts and minds. That way, when worry comes around, we're prepared for it.

Second, we must keep our focus where it should be. As Christians, we are running a race, and our focus should be on the finish line, not on the obstacles we have to deal with before we get there. We must keep our eyes on God! This is accomplished best by following the advice in I Thessalonians 5:17, *Pray without ceasing.*

If we stay in constant communion with God, we'll discover that worry no longer bothers us. But when we get too busy to talk with God, the "worry train" comes chugging down the track, beckoning us to climb aboard. It's not worth it. We must immerse ourselves in God's Word and in

fellowship with Him. It's our only hope of
avoiding the "worry train."

MIRACLE GRO FOR BITTERNESS?

How long does it take for a seed to become a beautiful flower? How long does it take for an acorn to become a growing oak? How long does it take for a root of bitterness to overcome all senses? Not as long as you would think!!!

I spotted that root of bitterness in my own life last week. My husband and I have had a tough year. Six months of unemployment have left us under a serious financial burden. I've prayed. I've cried. I've poured my heart out to God time and time again, yet things seem to only get worse. My faith has gotten weak, and my fear has grown by leaps and bounds.

I know that I am not the best at handling difficult situations. Jason just sits back and says, "God's in control. Everything will be fine." The thing is. . . he really means it. When I say that, what I'm really thinking is *Yes, God is in control, but He obviously needs my help on this one. What can I do to make this work?* My prayer day after day is "Lord, I believe. Help thou mine unbelief." I want to trust Him. I just can't seem to let go. I can't seem to hand the reins over to

Him. So, when things don't work out, I get frustrated. Lately, I've noticed my frustration turning to anger towards God. Like the disciples on the stormy seas, I've found myself shouting to the heavens, "God, don't you even care what's happening down here?"

I had no idea how deep my root of bitterness had grown until last Wednesday. We were sitting in the hospital waiting room during the surgery of a little girl from our church. Our pastor was telling us of a huge financial blessing he and his family had just received. Instead of being happy for them, I found myself thinking, *Lord, why won't you do that for us? We're good people too. We're serving you. We give when we don't have it to give. What more do you want?* (The Lord has given us unexpected blessings more than once, but it's hard to remember that in the middle of a pity party.) I'm happy to say that I immediately recognized my thought pattern for what it was and dismissed it. I apologized to the Lord and went on about my day.

Unfortunately, even though it had been dismissed, the root didn't go away. It stayed in my heart and continued to grow. For the next few days, I found myself mad at the world and

God. I honestly don't think I've ever been so low spiritually. I told Jason, "I understand now how people can turn their backs on God because it sure does seem like He's turned His back on me." I couldn't believe the words that were coming out of my mouth. What was even harder to believe was that I meant them. The Lord used Jason to straighten me out. He forced me to take a look at my life and to see the real problem. I knew what the problem was. I just didn't want to admit it. I have NOT been trusting God. I've been planning and scheming and doing everything I could think of to "help God out." The big problem with that is that I've been so busy "helping God" that I've forsaken my writing, the very thing He has called me to do. In essence, I felt God telling me, "If you'll do your part, I'll do my part." It seems so simple. Why was it so hard for me to get to that point? Bitterness!

I read once that bitterness is like drinking a poison and then waiting for the other person to die. That's an excellent description of bitterness! Beware, the root of bitterness can slip in without notice. Before long, you're dealing with an entire tree! We must be on guard.

Bitterness can ruin our lives and our walk with
God.

The heart knoweth his own bitterness; and a stranger doth not intermeddle with his joy. - Proverbs 14:10

NO DOUBT ABOUT IT - GOD IS GOOD!

Okay, remember a couple of days ago when I had that glorious little pity party? I was growing bitter because God was blessing others and I felt like He wasn't blessing me. Remember that? God has a way of straightening out His children.

First off, let me say that by the time I wrote that devotion, I had gotten things settled. The Lord and I had a LONG talk, and I was feeling much better. I apologized for my attitude and my behavior. I remembered all the ways the Lord had blessed me through the years. Everything was fine, but "fine" is not good enough for the Lord. Now that I had my act together, He wanted to remind me just how much He cares for me and how well He takes care of me.

On Tuesday, I went to the bank to make a well-needed deposit. For some reason, we were REALLY short on money and the mortgage payment was due. I was determined that morning that I wasn't going to worry about the fact that the deposit I was making was not as much as the mortgage payment. I was going to trust God. I had no idea how He was going to do it, but somehow, He would make ends meet.

I discovered that I didn't have a deposit slip, so I had to go into the bank. As I stood at the station filling out my deposit slip, I reached into my person to grab Jason's paycheck. You can imagine my surprise when I saw that there were two checks in my purse instead of one. *What in the world?* I thought, pulling out the second check. Evidently, in the craziness of last week with Kristen's surgery and everything, I had forgotten to make a deposit. I had not deposited Jason's check. . . the check that had several hours of overtime.

I laughed. I stood in the middle of the bank and laughed as tears filled my eyes. God had provided the money. In fact, it had been sitting in my purse for a week! I could almost hear the Lord say, "I am here, child, and I do care. All you have to do is trust me."

I couldn't wait to get out of the bank and call Jason. He laughed too. I went home and had a wonderful day because I realized that God cares enough about me to prove His love to me even when I don't deserve it. No doubt about it—God is good!

The LORD is good unto them that wait for him, to the soul that seeketh him. - Lamentations 3:25

NOT MEASURING UP

In Chapter 5 of the book of Daniel, King Belshazzar (Nebuchadnezzar's son) hosted a party. As if his party wasn't bad enough with all the drinking and sinful practices taking place, he commanded his servants to bring him the cups that his father had stolen from the temple (God's house). Not wise!

Not long after that, a hand appeared out of thin air. (I'm sorry, but that would probably scare me to death.) Belshazzar was pretty scared too. The Bible says, *Then the king's countenance was changed, and his thoughts troubled him, so that the joints of his loins were loosed, and his knees smote one against another.* I'd say that's pretty scared.

You know the rest of the story. The hand wrote on the wall, "MENE, MENE, TEKEL, UPHARSIN." The king, at the advice of his wife, summoned Daniel to translate the meaning of the words. Daniel reminded Belshazzar of the time his father, Nebuchadnezzar, was removed from his throne and made to live like a beast of the field because of his pride. In "Dana jargon," this is what Daniel said next: "And you, Belshazzar, are doing the exact same thing as your father did, even though you know what happened to him. You've stolen from the house of God. You've drunk wine. You've worshipped idols. And above all, you've failed to praise the God who gave you the breath you need to stay alive. And so, your kingdom will be taken from you as well. You're done!"

The part I want to really focus on is the meaning of the word "TEKEL" that was written on the wall. Look at verse 27: *TEKEL; Thou art weighed in the balances, and art found wanting.*

Can you imagine hearing anything more heartbreaking than that? Can you imagine God coming to you and saying such a thing?

I pray that the Lord never has to tell me that I am found wanting. I pray, instead, that He will be able to say of me what He said of Daniel in the next chapter.

Then the presidents and princes sought to find occasion against Daniel concerning the kingdom; but they could find none occasion nor fault; forasmuch as he was faithful, neither was there any error or fault found in him. - Daniel 6:4

Please understand, this verse is not saying that Daniel was perfect. Only God is perfect. However, it is saying that he lived such a God-filled life that fault was not immediately evident. It means that he was not found wanting. It means that God was pleased with Daniel's faithfulness and integrity. It means that Daniel was striving to be like the Lord. It means Daniel was being a true Christian.

The word Christian literally means "Christ-like," but we often use the term simply to identify a believer. Sad to say, I've met a few believers who were not at all "Christ-like." If we're going to call ourselves Christians, we need to live up to that title. Otherwise, we are disobeying the third of the ten commandments. We are taking the name of the Lord in vain. We are flippantly saying that we are like Him, while at the same time living in our wickedness. At that point, the word "Christian" is just a title with little or no meaning. Let's be careful. God is watching. What will He be able to say about us?

It's time to stop straddling the fence. Are we on His side or not? If so, let's act like it so that when the world looks at us, they'll have to look really hard to find fault. And during that time of observation, who knows, they may be blinded by the Son!

LEARNING TO BE WATCHFUL

Last Saturday, we took our youth group to the home of some shut-ins to do yard work. This elderly couple has severe health problems, and we thought it would be a good thing for the youth to learn the joy of doing for others. So, we gathered rakes and attempted to rake up their yard and clean out their gutters. Notice I said "attempted."

They have several large trees in their yard, and the more we raked, the more the wind blew. At times, it was downright frustrating. We hadn't been there long when one of the other youth leaders found a baby copperhead hiding in the leaves. I DON'T LIKE SNAKES!!!!! After the guys studied the squirming creature for a few minutes, they cut off its head. Yuck! I went around and warned all the other groups to be careful.

I had been carelessly scooping up leaves by the handfuls up until that point, but after seeing that snake, I was much more cautious about what I was picking up. It was a good thing because the pile I was working on was full of giant spiders. I

DON'T LIKE SPIDERS EITHER!!!! Then, to top it all off, I was on the last little bit of the pile when a lovely little scorpion came crawling out. At that point, our youth group had the opportunity to see me dance. I don't know how many times I stomped on that thing, but my feet were sore when I was done. I REALLY DON'T LIKE SCORPIONS!!!!!!!!! I was stung by one once, and I never want to experience that again. So, needless to say, we had a VERY interesting day, and I even learned a couple of things.

1.) Sometimes it seems like your work is in vain, but just keep trying. There were still leaves on the ground when we left. They were falling from the trees every second. Despite that, the yard looked much better when we left than it had when we arrived. Was it clear of leaves? No. Was it much better? Yes. So, was the work in vain? No, it just seemed like it at the time.

2.) It's wise to be on guard. If we hadn't found the snake to begin with, I wouldn't have been nearly as careful, and I could have been bitten by a spider or stung by a scorpion. But because I was on guard, I likely prevented some bad things from happening. Life is the same way. If we will be on guard, we might prevent some nasty falls.

Watch out for that dirty thought. Be on the lookout for that unkind word. Does that mean we won't mess up? No, but we have a better chance if we will learn to be watchful. Who knows? We may even get to do a little dance!

Therefore let us not sleep, as do others; but let us watch and be sober. - 1 Thessalonians 5:6

GOD CAN USE ANYBODY

Do you ever have a problem with Satan coming to you and telling you that God can't use you? You're too old. You're too young. You don't have enough experience. You don't have enough talent. You're not called. You've got too much sin in your past. You're just not good enough. Satan has a long list of lies that he uses to hinder us from doing the work of the Lord. The next time you feel that God can't use you, remember these facts about some noteworthy characters from the Bible (all of whom God used).

Rahab was a harlot.

David was an adulterer and murderer.

Jonah ran from God.

Abraham and Sarah were old enough to be great, great grandparents.

Samson had a weakness for a pretty face.

Solomon worshipped idols.

Matthew was a tax collector (aka thief).

Peter denied Christ.

Lazarus was dead.

Noah turned out to be a drunk.

Paul murdered Christians for a living.

Baalam's donkey was. . .well. . .a donkey!

The list could go on and on. Simply put, God can use anybody, anywhere, anytime!!!

Being confident of this very thing, that he which hath begun a good work in you will perform it until the day of Jesus Christ: - Philippians 1:6

DRIPPING WITH BLESSINGS

Last night when we got home from church, our dogs greeted us at the door just as they always do. We gave them some loving, and then headed to the kitchen for a snack. (Does anyone else get REALLY hungry during church?)

As I was looking through the refrigerator, I noticed there was only a small amount of milk in the container. We had a new jug of milk, so I thought the remainder of the first container would be a nice little treat for the dogs. They love milk! So, I poured a little into each of their bowls, and they drank greedily.

As they were drinking, Jason and I found a snack and began eating as we stood at the kitchen counter. Mitch, having finished his milk, came in and sat in front of Jason. With the most convincing look he could muster, he stared at Jason pitifully. I made some comment about the "poor starving puppy." Jason replied, "Yeah, his act would be much more convincing if he didn't still have milk dripping from his chin." I laughed, but then a hidden message hit me.

I do the same thing. I go to God with my "wish list." I look to Him with my poor-pitiful-me eyes. "I need this. I need that. I lack so many things," I tell Him. Little do I realize that I have blessings dripping from me. I don't NEED anything. I WANT a lot of things, but that's not the same thing. It is so easy to get into the frame of mind that I've been done wrong. Do you ever feel like that?

They have the job I want. **They** have money. **They** have a nice car. **They** live in a nice house. **They** have this, and **they** have that. I don't have any of that stuff, boo hoo! What a load of nonsense, but I fall for it time and time again. How dare I stand before God demanding more when I have blessings dripping from my chin!

Thankfully, God is a very patient and under-standing God. Still, I don't want to be ungrateful for the many ways that He's blessed me. I don't want to ever lose sight of all that He's done for me. I pray that I will never forget, and that I will ever be mindful of the blessings I've received.

If you have enjoyed this book, you'll love my blog, *A Word Fitly Spoken*. Go to http://DanaRongione.blogspot.com. You can even sign up to have the posts sent to you via e-mail. This is a free service, so be sure to sign up today to receive your daily dose of encouragement.

Made in the USA
Middletown, DE
15 July 2017